The Nature of Consciousness

The Nature of Consciousness

A Hypothesis

Susan Pockett

Writers Club Press
San Jose New York Lincoln Shanghai

The Nature of Consciousness
A Hypothesis

Published by Writers Club Press
an imprint of iUniverse.com, Inc.

For information address:
iUniverse.com, Inc.
620 North 48th Street
Suite 201
Lincoln, NE 68504-3467
www.iuniverse.com

ISBN: 0-595-12215-9

Printed in the United States of America

PREFACE

This book is written to put forward a particular scientific hypothesis about the nature of conscious experiences, or qualia. It is aimed largely at academic readers, but because of the wide variety of professional backgrounds among academics interested in the nature of consciousness, I have tried to write so that the argument will be clear to anyone with a high school education in general science and an interest in one of the oldest questions of humankind: "what is mind?" Despite this good intention however, there are probably some parts of the text that will be incomprehensible to anyone without a reasonably solid background in neurophysiology. I have tried to help at these points by including a small amount of Beginner's Guide type material as appendices.

It should be said at the outset that at the time of writing, the hypothesis I advance here is not, as far as I know, accepted by anyone in the academic world of consciousness studies (with the obvious exception of myself). Therefore the book is organized as a polemic. First the basic hypothesis is introduced and its origins in ancient philosophy are shown. Then some ground rules for discussion are laid and a considerable amount of neurophysiological evidence supporting the hypothesis is given. In the light of this supporting evidence the hypothesis is expanded beyond its basic statement. Further empirical evidence is then given to show that the idea explains not only how the brain affects consciousness, but also how consciousness affects the brain. Next, a number of objections to the hypothesis are stated and refuted. Finally, some rather large implications of the idea are sketched briefly.

So what is this controversial hypothesis? The basic question it goes to is that most ancient of philosophical saws, the mind-body problem. The mind-body problem boils down to the question of whether consciousness (mind) is a physical phenomenon or a non-physical one. The position that consciousness is a physical phenomenon is known as materialism and the position that it isn't is called dualism. Almost all modern-day scientists are, at least on the surface, fierce materialists. Indeed in scientific circles these days the word "dualist" is so unacceptable that it tends to be reserved as a last-ditch imprecation, to be hurled only when all else has failed to dispose of an opponent's argument. However, to many philosophers, the materialist position that is so much an article of faith among scientists simply fails to satisfy. The argument against it is essentially an intuitive one—mind and matter just seem to be different classes of phenomena. In fact, even to many scientists this privately seems an intuition with much to recommend it, but the problem remains that those in the anti-materialist camp who bite the bullet and frankly espouse dualism do have a hard time explaining how something that is not itself material could affect matter in the brain (as consciousness must if it is to influence the behavior of those who possess it). This difficulty sometimes leads to the intuitively bizarre position that consciousness actually doesn't affect matter in the brain at all —that it is merely an epiphenomenon, with no causal powers in the material world. No wonder this is such a long-running debate. However, all is not lost—into this mess rides the hypothesis put forward here.

The essence of the present hypothesis can be stated in one sentence. It is that **consciousness is identical with certain spatiotemporal patterns in the electromagnetic field.**

Now if this hypothesis is true, it may not be overstating the case to say that it solves the mind-body problem at a stroke. If the hypothesis is true, then consciousness is not material in the usually accepted sense, but neither is it some kind of non-physical spook (which, being non-physical, is therefore not accessible to scientific investigation). Consciousness (or at least normal human consciousness) is a local, brain-generated, configuration of, or pattern in, the electromagnetic field. A brain-sized spatial pattern in the electromagnetic field is not matter as such, so the hypothesis escapes the main objection to materialism. However, the electromagnetic field does have the easily observed property of affecting matter, so the hypothesis also side-steps the main objection to dualism. Philosophically speaking, this looks like a winner.

But the question remains, is it just another philosophical speculation, or is this a hypothesis supported by the vast mass of presently available scientific evidence on consciousness? The major part of the present book is an argument that the central hypothesis *is* supported by a great deal of empirical evidence, and thus that it must be considered a serious scientific hypothesis, deserving of further experimental investigation.

The structure of the book is as follows.

The introduction introduces. Chapter 1 sets down some working definitions and a set of criteria by which to evaluate scientific evidence on the neural correlates of consciousness. Chapters 2 to 5 lay out a considerable body of perfectly standard and reputable neuroscientific data showing that both the different states of consciousness (i.e. waking, sleeping and dreaming) and the specific sensory experiences of waking consciousness (i.e olfactory, auditory and visual experiences), are indeed associated with identifiable electromagnetic patterns generated by the brain. Chapter 6 fleshes out the hypothesis in more detail and names it *the electromagnetic field theory of consciousness*. It also points out that sensible answers fall naturally out of the theory to at least two questions which have previously been intractable: the question of what distinguishes the tiny fraction of brain activity that is available to consciousness at any given moment from the large proportion that is not, and another widely bothersome philosophical question called the binding problem. The differences between the present theory and the psychoneural identity theory are also discussed, the main difference being that the present theory predicts biological neurons to be in principle not necessary for the generation of conscious experience. The electromagnetic field theory of consciousness predicts that the right sorts of patterns in the electromagnetic field will be conscious, whatever generates them. Some practical consequences of this prediction and a possible empirical test of the theory which follows from the prediction are noted.

Chapter 7 moves on from the question of how the brain generates consciousness to a consideration of how consciousness acts back on its own brain. First the history of the idea that electromagnetic fields influence brain activity is given, and then current empirical evidence that they do so on a routine basis, as part of the normal operation of the brain, is presented. Chapter 8 then considers six different objections to the theory and provides answers to them. Finally, Chapter 9 discusses the relationships between this theory and the ideas of Charles Darwin, the experiences of mystics through the ages and commonly held notions about a universal consciousness, also known as God.

It is probably superfluous to say that I think the central idea put forward here is an important one, which deserves to be further investigated on a large-scale basis. My hope is that this monograph will convince you of the importance of the idea too, dear reader, and that it may even inspire some bushy-tailed young graduate students of the future to stake their careers on investigating the electromagnetic field theory of consciousness. However, whether or not the book succeeds in these lofty aims, I hope that you will at least find it a entertaining read.

Susan Pockett
Auckland, New Zealand
December 1999

INTRODUCTION

❖ Aim of this book—History of the atomic theory of matter—Ancient views about consciousness—A hypothesis on the nature of consciousness

Aim of this book

The aim of this book is to lay the foundation stone for a scientific theory of the nature of conscious experience.

When I first started thinking seriously on this question about five years ago, I had no clue as to what such a theory would look like. All I did know was that in order to be counted as scientific, it would have to have certain characteristics. It would have to fit all the available empirical evidence on the relationship of consciousness to the brain. It would probably have to be potentially falsifiable by new experimental evidence (although the theory of evolution, which must be one of the most successful scientific theories of all time, sits rather uneasily with that criterion). And most daunting of all, it would probably have to involve some sort of new fundamental principle about the universe. These seemed fairly onerous requirements.

However, being a New Zealander and thus imbued from childhood with the notion that I was a rugged individualist who could fix anything with a piece of number eight fencing wire, I was not as daunted by these obstacles as a more socialized person might have been, and simply made a start somewhere. On the principle that successful strategies can often be generalized, it seemed that a useful way to begin might be to look at the development of a successful theory in another area of science. Perhaps this would afford some ideas about how to proceed in the present case. Since what I was trying to build was a theory of the nature of mind, I decided that the currently accepted theory on the nature of matter might be a good starting point. So I began by taking a look at the history of the atomic theory.

History of the atomic theory of matter

It turned out that the idea that matter is composed of atoms was first put forward by the Greek philosopher Leucippus and his pupil Democritus, around 450 BC (Whyte, 1961). These thinkers were concerned to explain the observed fact that material objects change, while at the same time preserving a certain faith in the permanence of things that are real. Their speculation was that the universe consists of ultimate, indivisible atoms, each of them hard, permanent and unchangeable, of one homogenous substance but of various shapes and sizes. The atoms of fire, for example, were postulated to be smooth spheres. Atoms were conceived as being in constant motion, vibrating and whirling, though sometimes fitted together in stable combinations. All the variety of the universe was seen as resulting from the differences in size, shape, position, order and motion of these atoms of a single substance.

It must be said that this was an inspired and brilliant speculation. However, since it was philosophical rather than scientific in the sense in which we now understand science, it was subject to defeat of an almost political nature by other philosophical ideas. Plato and Aristotle did not much like it and its popularity declined, until by about 200 BC atomism as a philosophy was pretty much dead. The writings of Epicurus (341–270 BC) were influential in preserving the idea however, as were those of Asclepiades, a Greek physician in Rome who ascribed disease to alterations in the size, arrangement and motion of atoms in the body. Lucretius (98–55 BC), whose poem "De Rerum Natura" eloquently expressed the Democritan doctrine, was another supporter.

Atomistic ideas arose again, a century or so later, in India. The notion was probably independently conceived, although Kanada (the traditional name of whoever wrote the Hindu Vaisesika Sutras, probably sometime during the first two centuries AD) might have heard of Greek ideas on the subject. In any case, Vaisesika philosophy is explicitly atomistic. Unlike the myriad of Greek atoms, however, Kanada's atoms were conceived to be of only four different kinds: earth, water, fire and air. They were imagined as uniting to form dyads, triads and so on, building up to give rise to the universe.

Indian ideas were probably not much known in the West at that stage, but over the next thousand or so years the atomistic ideas of the Greeks kept being revived by various Arab and European thinkers—and kept being vigorously opposed by the Christian church. In fact for reasons that are not entirely clear the Paris Parliament went so far in 1624 as to decree that any person maintaining or teaching atomism, or any other doctrine contrary to Aristotle, would be put to death! Despite this somewhat heavy-handed approach (or knowing scientists, perhaps even because of it) atomism became the dominant theory of matter from around 1630 onwards. Between 1646 and 1691 at least seven European scientists, including Boyle, Leeuwenhoek, Newton and Halley, made or discussed experimentally based estimates of an upper limit for the size of atoms. Huygens even put forward a comprehensive quantitative theory based on atomic motion, which he applied to gravitation, atmospheric pressure, light (as waves of particle vibrations) and cohesion. Newton also proposed a corpuscular theory of light, with the motion of the corpuscles being guided by waves (in somewhat stunning anticipation of the latest theories on the nature of light). However this enthusiasm for atomism waned again and the 18th century was a relatively quiet period in the history of the idea. It was not until the chemists of the 19th century appeared on the scene that modern scientific atomism was really born.

By 1807, a good deal of experimentation in the emerging field of chemistry had produced the rather grandly named Law of Definite Proportions, which stated that for any given chemical compound, the constituent elements are always combined in the same proportions by weight, however the compound is made. A hypothesis explaining this was now proposed by Francis Dalton (who thereby became known among chemists as "the father of atomism"). Dalton suggested (a) that there exist invisible atoms (b) that those of any given element are alike in weight and those of different elements have different weights and (c) that atoms combine in a simple whole-number ratios to form compounds. While these were not ideas of any great originality, they were a clear set of experimentally testable postulates about the existence and nature of atoms (which, in the light of another couple of centuries of experimentation we now know were not all completely correct). The postulates were generated to explain specific experimental observations and they were immediately tested against more experimental observations.

Now there is a great deal more to the history of atomism, but this much will suffice to make a couple of important points:

(a) the basic idea that matter is composed of atoms arose at least twice in ancient philosophy.

(b) the eventual scientific version of the atomic theory was generated to explain specific experimental data.

How can we use these insights in the construction of a theory of consciousness? It is probably fair to say that at the close of the twentieth century we are in rather worse position with regard to a theory of consciousness than were the pre-Dalton chemists of the nineteenth century with regard to a theory of matter. That is to say, we have a large volume of experimental data, but really no simple, universal idea that ties it all together in a satisfactory way. So, by analogy with the atomic theory, perhaps we should look to the ancient philosophies of India and Greece for such an idea.

Ancient views about consciousness

On the nature of matter, we have seen that both the ancient Greeks and the ancient Hindus developed a very specific (and as time showed, substantially correct) theory. On the nature of consciousness however, it turns out that the Indian tradition has far more to say than the Greek.

The three basic texts in the Vedic tradition of India are the Upanishads, the Bhagavad-gita and the Brahma-sutra. Remarkably in view of their differing and sometimes fiercely argued views on other issues, all of these texts hold the same view of the nature of consciousness. This is that the world-ground—the sole and whole cause of the world and the universal Self, of which our individual selves are only parts—is an all-pervading pure consciousness or intelligence. This is called Brahman in the Brahma-sutra and the Bhagavad-gita (Maharishi, 1969) and either Brahman or Atman in those books of the Upanishads where it is mentioned (namely the Brhadaranyaka Upanishad and the Isa Upanishad). Pure conscious-ness—that is, consciousness without any object or subject—is held to be not an attribute of Atman/Brahman, but its essence. Various meditative techniques are presented more or less clearly in the various works, by use of which it is said to be possible to obtain direct experience of this field of pure consciousness, (as it is routinely translated from the Sanskrit). Such experience is reported to be the ultimate bliss, beyond which nothing else could ever be desired. Apart from blissfulness, the main characteristic of the universal consciousness is that it is all-pervading.

Let us move on now to the notions on consciousness propounded by the ancient Greek philosophers. Plato is uniformly regarded as being one of the greatest of these, and although as we have just seen he did get it wrong when it came to atomism, it turns out that he may have been more successful on the matter of consciousness. In fact it has been suggested, with considerable textual justification (Shear, 1990), that Plato independ-ently discovered a technique which allowed him to experience what the Vedic tradition calls Brahman. This technique is poorly described in

Plato's writings (as indeed are meditation techniques in the Vedas) and it has hitherto been regarded by modern philosophers as pretty much incomprehensible. The name given to it by Plato is generally translated from the Greek as "the dialectic". As a result of using his dialectic, Plato describes transcendental experiences of what he calls the Good, the Beautiful, or true Being, which bear a startling similarity to Vedic descriptions of the experience of Brahman. Plato's theory of Forms is tied to this transcendental or "after-death" realm, in which experience first of what he calls "an open sea of beauty" and then of "an eternal oneness", an "inviolable whole", simply pure, unbounded loveliness itself, is taken as being the experience of the Form of Beauty.

Plato's best-known pupil was Aristotle. While Aristotle was sharply critical of his teacher's theory of Forms in general and rejected their independent existence, he did make an exception in the case of the Form he variously called "Active Intelligence", the "Unmoved Mover", the "Good" and "God". Aristotle's doctrine of "psychological hylomorphism" (Modrak, 1987) posits the *psuche* (mind/soul) as being "the form of the body" and is presented by Aristotle as a genuine alternative to both reductive materialism and dualism. It can be interpreted in a number of different ways, but inasmuch as the modern notion of a field in physics is in some sense physical but not material, it is perhaps reasonable to suggest that Aristotle's hylomorphic notions with regard to consciousness could be read in terms of some sort of field. It must be admitted this is a tenuous interpretation and it is not clear whether it was the one intended by Aristotle himself—but then the whole idea of a field in the sense in which modern physics uses the term was unknown at the time. Aristotle's best known hypothesis about consciousness is that there exists a "common sense", which has the function of integrating information from the five specific senses into a unified perception of the world. Again, Aristotle did not specifically suggest that this common sense had the properties of a field (possibly because the concept of a field in this sense arose only with Faraday and James Clark Maxwell in the nineteenth century). However, as will be seen in later chapters, a field could certainly have the properties of the common sense.

In summary, although there is some lack of clarity here and the above interpretations are not at this stage standard among contemporary scholars, Greek thought may in general terms be read as being similar to Vedic thought on the subject of consciousness, just as it was on the subject of matter. In both Vedic and Platonic thought, it is held that some gifted or well-trained individuals are capable of directly experiencing an unbounded field of consciousness that is (a) pure consciousness without any contents in terms of thought or sensory experiences and (b) essentially infinite in time and space—or at any rate larger than the normal waking individual consciousness, which seems to be confined inside an individual's head.

A hypothesis on the nature of consciousness

The closest modern physics comes to the idea of an all-pervading, nondual entity is probably the notion of the unified field. Indeed, one contemporary commentator on the Vedas, Maharishi Mahesh, has already equated Brahman-Atman with the unified field (Hagelin, 1984). However the concept of a unified field is itself in a very preliminary stage of formulation at this point, so it may be more fruitful for our purposes to examine one particular manifestation of the unified field which has a quite direct, empirically-measurable relationship with working brains. This is the electromagnetic field. The electromagnetic field is just as all-pervading as the putative unified field, and it holds for us the distinct charm that its configurations are already routinely measured by both clinical and research neurophysiologists, throughout the world and on a daily basis. Consequently, we already have a huge mass of data on the relationship of various configurations of the electromagnetic field to the phenomenology of consciousness.

So perhaps the answer we have been looking for is that what has in the past been called the electromagnetic field is itself conscious. And perhaps our individual consciousnesses, which unlike the field as a whole *are* bounded in space and time, are identical with particular local spatiotemporal configurations of the electromagnetic field.

At first sight, this idea may seem outrageous or even bizarre. After all, every basic physics text lays out the properties of the electromagnetic field, and consciousness is not one of them. Manifestations of the electromagnetic field include radio waves, light, X-rays and gamma rays. None of these has anything whatsoever to do with consciousness. What are can we be thinking, to propose that the electromagnetic field is conscious? Surely this is nothing more than New Age mumbo jumbo?

On closer consideration however, the idea is not as upsetting as it may at first appear. All of the mentioned varieties of waves in the electromagnetic field (light, radio waves and so on) have frequencies above a thousand cycles per second (see Table 1) and there exists a whole spectrum of frequencies lower than this range for which no particular properties have been assigned. In particular, the extremely low frequency (ELF) range of electromagnetic fluctuations from 0 to 100 Hz has not attracted too much interest from physicists until now (probably because waves of this frequency do not propagate well and are therefore not particularly useful for transmitting information over long distances). Interestingly, 0 to 100 Hz turns out to be exactly the frequency range of the electromagnetic oscillations that are generated by biological brains.

So perhaps this idea does deserve further consideration. Perhaps it will even turn out to be the basis for an answer to the so-called Hard Questions (Chalmers, 1996): "Why does conscious experience exist? If it arises from physical systems, as seems likely, how does it arise? Is consciousness itself physical, or is it merely a concomitant of physical systems? How widespread is consciousness? Do mice, for example, have conscious experiences?...Why is seeing red like *this*, rather than like *that*? Why...do we experience the reddish sensation that we do, rather than some entirely different kind of sensation, like the sound of a trumpet?" Perhaps it will answer the call of the same author, when he says "Ultimately one would like a theory of consciousness to do at least the following: it should give conditions under which physical processes give rise to consciousness, and for those processes that give rise to consciousness, it should specify just what sort of experience is associated. And we would like the theory to explain *how* it arises, so that the emergence of consciousness seems intelligible rather than magical. In the end, we would like the theory to enable us to see consciousness as an integral part of the natural world. Currently it may be hard to see what such a theory would be like, but without such a theory we could not be said to fully understand consciousness."

Let us see if we can show Dr Chalmers what such a theory would be like.

Table 1: Accepted and proposed properties of regions of the electromagnetic spectrum.

REGION OF THE ELECTROMAGNETIC SPECTRUM	FREQUENCY (Hz)
Gamma ray	10^{21}–10^{24}
X ray	10^{18}–10^{20}
Ultraviolet light	10^{15}–10^{16}
Visible light	4–7×10^{14}
Infrared light	10^{12}–10^{14}
Microwave	10^{10}–10^{11}
Radio wave	10^{4}–10^{11}
Consciousness	0–10^{2}

CHAPTER ONE: GROUND RULES

The nature of explanation in science

In science, the nature of explanation is most often such that some empirical phenomenon is considered explained if it can be related to previously established fundamental principles. For example, the motion of a baseball is explained at the beginning of the 21st century in terms of the force imparted by the pitcher's arm, the resistance of the atmosphere, the air turbulence caused by the spin of the ball and, most of all, in terms of the force of gravity. But what about the situation in 1620 with regard to the explanation of the motion of planets? It is technically true to say that Newton "explained" planetary motion in terms of the fundamental principle of gravitational attraction, but "explained" has a subtly different sense here. The principle of gravitation, or at least its universality, was actually being established by Newton's explanation of the motion of planets. So in this case, Newton was not relating a single empirical phenomenon to previously established fundamental principles; he was relating several otherwise independent phenomena (Kepler's three laws of planetary motion) to a common underlying principle which thereby *became* established.

In other words, when there are already established fundamental principles in an area, an empirical phenomenon is considered to be explained if it can be related to these fundamental principles. But if there are no fundamental principles already established, such principles must first come to be established. The way this generally happens is that the fundamental principles are first proposed and then shown to be valid by showing that they explain many otherwise unrelated observations.

In essence, what this book is doing is proposing a basic fundamental scientific principle regarding consciousness and then seeking to establish this principle, by showing that it explains many observations.

The basic fundamental principle being proposed here is that consciousness is identical with certain spatiotemporal patterns in the electromagnetic field.

At this stage we can say nothing about the shape of these spatio-temporal electromagnetic patterns or the nature of the rules that connect such patterns with subjective experience. Those details will come later. What we need to do first is try and establish the truth of the basic fundamental principle that certain spatiotemporal electromagnetic patterns are identical with conscious experiences.

The analysis above about how fundamental principles are generally established in science would suggest that all we need do is come up with some measured electromagnetic field patterns that always covary with conscious experiences. If we can do this, we should have established our fundamental principle, by showing that it does tie together all the observations that have so far been made (and that there is reasonable hope that it will tie together observations yet to be made) about conscious experiences. An optimist, or indeed a historian of science, might well accept this proposal.

However, suppose we did find that certain spatiotemporal patterns in the electromagnetic field always covary with particular conscious experiences. What would be the actual effect of this on the minds of real-life scientists? There are basically two possible interpretations of such a finding:

(a) the patterns themselves are identical with conscious experiences

(b) the patterns are meaningless epiphenomena generated in a more or less lawful way by the workings of the brain, which workings are themselves either conscious experience *per se* (the psychoneural identity theory) or necessary to produce whatever conscious experiences really are (varieties of dualism).

The attitude of most physiologists towards the brain-generated electromagnetic patterns that can be measured by EEG recording has traditionally been option (b)—that they are meaningless epiphenomena, merely the smoke produced by the fire of brain activity. This view was strongly held by the charismatic neurophysiological pioneer Sir John Eccles, who was very influential in promulgating the idea that the most important thing for physiologists to study was activity in single cells and synapses. Oddly enough the other arm of Eccles' beliefs about the mind, which was essentially dualist, is now held by physiologists (who in general subscribe to the psychoneural identity theory) to be downright heretical—but his influence in the matter of the epiphenomenality of the EEG has remained strong.

On the other hand, the view in disciplines other than neurophysiology has traditionally been much more open to the idea that electromagnetic patterns have a direct ontological relationship with consciousness. In general this view is tenable (though never expressed openly) in university departments of physics and engineering and also in departments of psychiatry, probably because the human EEG was discovered by the psychiatrist Hans Berger.

The other group of scientists who one would have thought should have a professional interest in consciousness are psychologists. However oddly enough, psychologists in the century or so after William James became completely sidetracked by the Behaviorist paradigm into believing that consciousness didn't actually exist at all, or at least that it was not to be mentioned in polite academic company, and it is only relatively recently that the cognitive revolution has restored consciousness to the status of a fit subject for study in psychology departments. As a result of this strange situation, for some decades a knowledge of brain structure and function was not deemed necessary for the study of psychology. Perhaps because of their relatively recent conversion to the opposite viewpoint, cognitive psychologists today tend to be more inclined to the neurophysiological approach to the study of mind i.e. either to take for granted some version of the neural identity theory, or to be functionalists who see consciousness as a process rather than any form of substance.

So, reaction to a finding that there is a strong correlation between electromagnetic patterns and consciousness is likely to be split fairly cleanly along disciplinary lines (with of course, a few honorable exceptions). Some will accept the possibility that correlation in this case indicates identity, but rather more will naturally adopt the opposite viewpoint. Rather than plunge into the philosophical swamp on this issue, let us just flag it as a potential problem and set it aside. The first thing to determine is whether or not there do actually exist patterns in the electromagnetic field which carry all the necessary information for distinguishing, from the outside so to speak, one experience from another. In other words, the question is, do there exist electromagnetic patterns which reliably predict the existence of particular conscious experiences? If there do, then the philosophical question of identity may become worth discussing.

Definitions and rules of evidence

In order to answer the question of whether or not there actually exist the sorts of correlations between conscious experience and electromagnetic patterns which we are looking for, we must first lay down some working definitions and also some ground rules for acceptability of experimental evidence.

Consciousness

The definition of the word consciousness has stopped in their tracks more academic discussions than you could shake a stick at. It would be possible to write a whole book on the subject of the definition of the word consciousness (and indeed in some senses this is exactly what the current book is about). But whatever our conclusions may turn out to be at the end of this exercise, clearly some attempt must be made at the outset to state as plainly as possible what it is that we are talking about.

Perhaps the obvious first step is to consult a dictionary for a definition of consciousness. The Pocket Oxford Dictionary at first appears to be admirably concise on the subject. It says that the noun "consciousness" means "awareness; person's conscious thoughts and feelings as a whole". Unfortunately this is impression of precision is rather spoiled when one looks up the adjective "aware" and finds that it means "conscious". Clearly there is no help to be had from this source, other than the information that the words conscious and aware are generally regarded as being synonymous.

Where to now? Since words are the stock in trade of philosophers, perhaps we should see what philosophers have to say about the definition of the word conscious. John Searle offers the following (Searle, 1993):

"Like most words, "consciousness" does not admit of a definition in terms of genus and differentia or necessary and sufficient conditions. Nonetheless, it is important to say exactly what we are talking about, because the phenomenon of consciousness that we are interested in needs to be distinguished from certain other phenomena such as attention, knowledge and self-consciousness. By "consciousness", I simply mean those subjective states of sentience or awareness that begin when one wakes up in the morning from a dreamless sleep and continue throughout the day until one goes to sleep at night or falls into a coma, or dies, or otherwise becomes, as one would say, "unconscious"."

This definition is fine in that it does basically tell us what we are talking about, but not terribly satisfactory in that it says nothing about how one might determine whether or not an entity other than ourselves is conscious. The classical Turing test (which basically defines an entity as intelligent if it is not possible to distinguish between it and another human in casual conversation) can clearly be passed by simple computer programs which no-one would accept as being conscious in the same sense as humans are, but would not be passed by great apes, to which most people would be inclined to grant the possession of at least simple consciousness. Unfortunately however, there appears to be no better test for the presence of another consciousness available at this time. My own preference is simply to sidestep the issue, by saying only that I know what conscious experience means in my own case and I infer from your behavior and the fact that you look roughly like me that it means something similar for you, dear reader (although I can never actually be sure of that).

Simple, self and cosmic consciousness

One further refinement of the definition of consciousness which may be useful is provided by the psychiatrist Richard Maurice Bucke. In his classic description of mystical experience (Bucke, 1993), this author divides consciousness into three types or grades: simple consciousness, self consciousness and cosmic consciousness. Simple consciousness is possessed by humans and also by animals such as cats and dogs—it consists largely of sensory experiences and perceptions. Humans usually make the transition at some time in their childhood from simple consciousness to self consciousness, which is possessed by all normal adult persons. This consists of a state in which one is aware that one is an individual, a self. Cosmic consciousness is described by Bucke as a further state, which has been attained by only a few humans in the history of the race (although the author suggests that the number with this faculty is increasing over the centuries) and almost never appears before the age of about 35. It consists of an ongoing, direct awareness that one is not actually an individual after all, but merely part of an all-encompassing, immortal Self. The stereotypic mystical experience in which this is realised for the first time is generally called the unity experience. That cosmic consciousness is not merely a pathological state is evidenced by the major accomplishments in science and the arts of those whose writings suggest they experienced it.

The main part of this book is about simple consciousness, which consists of sensory experiences. So unless otherwise specified, the word consciousness will hereafter be used to mean simple consciousness. However it will be seen in the last chapter that the theory expounded here about the nature of consciousness just as easily incorporates or provides an explanation for cosmic consciousness.

States and contents of consciousness

In thinking about simple consciousness, is convenient to distinguish between general states of consciousness and specific contents of consciousness. The term "states of consciousness" is usually taken to refer to the states of waking, sleeping and dreaming. The absolute minimum that must be done by any theory of consciousness worth its salt is to explain the difference between these major states. As will be seen in Chapter 2, the electromagnetic theory of consciousness eats this requirement for breakfast.

The term "contents of consciousness" refers to the multitude of specific subjective experiences that occur during the states of waking and dreaming. A good theory of consciousness must also make transparent this enormous variety of subjective experiences. This is a much more difficult requirement to fulfill, in part simply because of the vastness of the number of experiences that need to be accommodated. Naturally the electromagnetic theory of consciousness has to work somewhat harder here, but we'll see what it can do.

Rules of evidence

Requirements for identifying an electromagnetic pattern with a specific subjective experience

Simple sensory experiences are probably the easiest kinds of subjective experiences to study, because they have some more-or-less direct relationship with the external world, which allows us to manipulate them experimentally in a more-or-less objective way. Therefore, it may be advantageous to start by searching for common underlying electromagnetic patterns which correlate with sensory experiences. To limn what we are looking for, this may be one or more general electromagnetic patterns that occur across all sensory modalities (with appropriate differences between the senses so that each sensory modality can be understood as generating qualitatively different conscious experiences) plus some more specific spatiotemporal patterns that can be used as building blocks to generate the myriad of different possible specific sensory experiences.

These specific electromagnetic patterns must have a number of characteristics that tie them to sensory experiences:

1.1 The electromagnetic patterns must be present when and only when particular experiences can be reported by the experimental subject as being conscious. In practical terms, this means that:

(i) The electromagnetic pattern must be present when the sensory experience under study can be reported by the subject and must cease to be present at the exact moment when the experience ceases to be present during

(a) removal of the physical stimulus

(b) shutting off of the peripheral sense organs (closing the eyes, stopping the ears)

(c) turning down of the physical stimulus below the threshold for sensation

(d) habituation to repetitive stimuli

(e)   induction of anesthesia

(f)   onset of sleep

(g)   cessation of the sensation due to selective attention to something else

(h)   cessation of the sensation due to binocular or binaural rivalry

(ii) The electromagnetic pattern must not be present in cases of

(a)   congenital sensory deficit, such as blindness or deafness

(b)   induced sensory deficit, such as that caused by neurological insults that destroy sensation (this criterion includes cases like blindsight, where some pre-conscious processing of sensory information is preserved, but conscious awareness of the stimulus is absent)

1.2 The electromagnetic patterns must co-vary with subjective experience (rather than with the physical stimulus)

(i)   in cases of "gestalt" perceptual illusions: eg the flipping of viewpoints experienced when viewing a Necker cube

(ii) as a sensation increases in magnitude when stimulus strength is turned up, according to the empirically established psychophysical laws (Appendix A)

(iii) when the subject comes to experience the stimulus differently, as when learning gives the stimulus a new "meaning" for the subject: e.g. the taste of a glass of red wine is experienced very differently by a novice wine-drinker than by the same person after they have spent years learning about wine-tasting—with experience, distinctions can be made which were literally impossible at the beginning. Similarly, a light or a tone is probably experienced differently by a rat depending on whether it has learned to associate this particular stimulus with food or a foot-shock.

1.3. The electromagnetic patterns should be generated by localized areas of the brain.

There are 3 reasons for specifying this as a criterion. First, the observation that localized *lesions* to various areas of the cortex cause discrete disturbances in the contents of consciousness has been made repeatedly ever since Paul Broca reported in 1861 that a small lesion in the third frontal convolution of the left hemisphere of the human brain produced loss of speech or aphasia, without other obvious disability (Broca, 1861). Secondly, *stimulation* of discrete areas of brain evokes memories of discrete conscious experiences. The first evidence of this was produced by Wilder Penfield and colleagues in the 1940s (Penfield & Rasmussen, 1968). During surgery to remove tumors or epileptic foci, these workers stimulated very localized sites on the surface of their awake patients' cerebral cortices and thus elicited reports both of very specific sensory experiences such as tingling in the left big toe, and more integrative experiences such as sensations of *déjà vu*, or of being outside one's body. Thirdly, the various recently invented techniques of *brain imaging* have repeatedly shown that discretely localized areas of brain are active during the experience of discrete contents of consciousness.

However, the above criterion notwithstanding,

1.4 The electromagnetic patterns should have a certain global quality, which in practical terms probably means that they should be available over a wide area of the brain.

The arguments for including global accessibility as a criterion are those put forward by Bernard Baars (Baars, 1988). First, conscious experience is normally unified and internally consistent. It seems to be impossible to see both interpretations of a Necker Cube at the same time, for example. Conscious perception is of a unified object, despite that fact that the neural encoding of the consciously perceived scene is distributed over a fairly large area of brain. Secondly, consciousness has a limited content at any one time, which means that conscious processes must act in serial (while unconscious processes can operate in parallel). At any given moment we are conscious of only a tiny fraction of the vast number of thoughts and perceptions that could potentially be flooding and completely overwhelming us. Thirdly, conscious processes tend to be inefficient and error-prone (as compared to the relative efficiency and accuracy of unconscious processes), but they are essential when faced with a novel situation. The metaphor used by Baars to explain all these observations is that there exists a "global workspace", which he equates with consciousness. Specialized neural processors are postulated to compete for access to this workspace, which is only functionally defined at this stage. Access to the workspace supposedly carries with it the ability to influence the overall direction in which the organism goes.

If we hypothesise that the realization of this postulated global workspace is a conscious electromagnetic field pattern (which in fairness it should be pointed out the originator of the global workspace concept did not, and at the time of writing still does not accept), then the above arguments imply two things. First, only a limited number of information-carrying electromagnetic patterns should be able to coexist in any given brain at any given time. These should be patterns that carry the information currently in conscious awareness. Secondly, there needs to be a demonstrable widespread effect of these electromagnetic patterns on neural processing, but this effect should only be a relatively inefficient and error prone one. Detailed computational work should still be done by subconscious, non-field-effect processes.

Methodological requirements

Above is one set of working criteria by which to judge whether or not certain electromagnetic patterns can be accepted as covarying with conscious experiences. The next step is to review the multitude of experiments already in the scientific literature, to see whether they fulfill the conditions specified for showing correlations between particular states or contents of consciousness and particular electromagnetic patterns generated by the brain. These experiments were probably not originally done with anything like the present hypothesis in mind, but nevertheless they may be the source of a great deal of relevant information. However, it is important to evaluate the experimental methods of these studies quite carefully to ensure that the reported findings are valid.

Broadly speaking there are two methods of measuring spatiotemporal electromagnetic patterns. First, such patterns may be measured by electroencephalographic (EEG) or magnetoencephalographic (MEG) studies, either on human subjects or on animals. EEG and MEG recordings deliver millisecond precision in the time domain, but spatial information is seriously corrupted or smeared by the volume conduction properties of the brain and skull, particularly for EEG measurements. Both techniques measure only contributions from sources that are oriented in a particular way with respect to the surface of the brain. Alternatively, albeit very much less efficiently in terms of patterns generated by the firing of many neurons, spatiotemporal electromagnetic patterns may be measured by multiple single cell recordings from the brains of animals. There are a number practical difficulties with both types of experiments, which must be overcome if the results are to be meaningful. The methodological requirements of neurocognitive studies designed to establish correlations between electromagnetic patterns and cognitive states have been discussed by a number of authors (Donchin, et al., 1977; Gevins, et al., 1985; Thatcher & John, 1977). They include:

(a)   Elimination of artefacts

Raw EEG and MEG recordings are easily contaminated by artefacts arising from muscle activity in the scalp or eye muscles. A particular difficulty is that lateral eye movements (saccades) and blinks have been shown to be correlated with cognitive processes (Just & Carpenter, 1976; Stern, Walrath, & Goldstein, 1984). Even instructions to avoid blinking can affect some task-related evoked potentials (Verleger, 1991). There are various methods in the literature for eliminating such artefacts, some more effective than others (Barlow, 1986).

Artefacts can also occur during the subsequent analysis of raw EEG data. One commonly used analysis method that is often contaminated by unrecognised methodological artefact is coherence analysis. Coherence measurements reflect the extent to which the oscillations of a particular frequency that are recorded at different electrode sites vary in concert. Being coherent in this sense is thus different from being in phase; e.g. 40 Hz oscillations recorded at two different sites can be out of phase, but still highly coherent if the phase difference between the two stays constant over time. Coherence is currently fashionable because it has recently been proposed as the factor that "binds" together the firing of individual neurons at widely dispersed sites in the brain to produce a single unified conscious percept. The pitfalls in coherence measurement relate largely to EEG recordings, which unlike intracellular recordings are highly dependent on the site of the reference electrode. A basic EEG recording measures the voltage difference between two electrodes, one of which is called the recording electrode and the other the reference electrode. In so-called monopolar recordings, the reference electrode is placed on an ear-lobe (or else a separate electrode is placed on each earlobe and the two are linked electrically) or on the mastoid bone behind the ear and it is therefore assumed that the reference electrode is inactive i.e. not affected by any electric fields produced by the brain. Unfortunately in practice, no reference site is inactive (Lehman, 1987), (with the possible exception of a non-cephalic or off-head reference, which is then likely to introduce new artefacts arising from the electrical activity of the heart). And depending on the particular reference site chosen, the reference electrode can itself contribute variation to both recordings which significantly influences measured coherence between a pair of electrodes (French & Beaumont, 1984). There are several explanations for the fact that empirically, coherence measurements do depend on the chosen reference (Beaumont & Rugg, 1979; Fein, Raz, Brown, & Merrin, 1988). To cope with this sort of problem, various strategies have been employed to convert EEG measurements to "reference-free" data. Using a computed average of recordings from all the electrodes as a virtual "average reference" is one such strategy, but a better one (because it also sharpens up spatial smearing due to volume conduction through brain and skull tissue) is the use of Laplacian derivatives. There are two main ways of deriving these mathematical transformations and each is subject to controversy (Nunez, et al., 1997). Life is never simple.

Another possible source of methodological artefact in the recording or analysis of EEG data is the overuse of frequency filters. In general, the wider the bandpass of filters the better, since an overly restrictive bandpass can introduce artefactual waveforms.

(b)   Control of general physiological factors

Brain signals vary with age, gender, handedness, fatigue, habituation, and use of caffeine, nicotine, alcohol and various other drugs. In general, these effects are fairly easy to control, but they must be taken into account. Level of autonomic arousal is another major factor to be considered. General arousal is rather difficult to control and its effects on the electromagnetic patterns generated by the brain are hard to separate out from more specific task-related effects (Kachaturian, Chisholm, & Kerr, 1973; Kachaturian & Gluck, 1969). Hence an attempt must be made to control such imprecisely specifiable factors as task difficulty and motivation.

(c)   Isolation of consciousness *per se* from other specific brain processes

By far the biggest methodological problem with studies designed to reveal the electromagnetic correlates of consciousness is the requirement to isolate the electromagnetic patterns associated with conscious experience from those associated with other brain processes. In general, the requirements for identifying electro-magnetic patterns with conscious experiences laid out in the pre-ceding section are aimed at ensuring that the electromagnetic patterns measured correlate with consciousness *per se* rather than with pre-conscious processing. However there are several issues on which the criteria specified might fall over.

(i)   The measured electromagnetic pattern may include some features that are not representative of the contents of con-sciousness, but instead are generated by pre-conscious neural processing events. It has been suggested that the best way to get around this problem is to compare the electromagnetic patterns generated by closely related pairs of cognitive states, one of which is conscious and the other of which is not (Baars, 1988). The rationale for this is presumably that the *difference* between the electromagnetic patterns associated with the closely related conscious and non-conscious states may be assumed to be the correlate of consciousness itself, while the *common features* of the two patterns will represent pre-conscious processing. It should be noted, however, that the assumptions underlying subtraction techniques likes one have been strongly criticized (Friston, et al., 1996).

(ii)   The measured electromagnetic pattern may correlate with some brain state that is merely coupled with a particular conscious experience for the purpose of experiment, such as preparation for a voluntary motor act used to communicate that the conscious experience is happening (like pushing a button, or vocalising). The best solution to this is probably to repeat the experiment using a different mode of communication and accept only those pattern aspects that correlate with the reported experience and not with the method of reporting. Even this strategy, however, may not eliminate certain generalised motor "readiness" potentials (McCallum, 1988).

(iii)   The measured electromagnetic pattern may correlate not with consciousness *per se*, but with something that always accompanies consciousness, such as the processes of voluntary or involuntary attention, or working memory (Baars, 1997b). This is by far the hardest of the three methodological problems mentioned in this section. It is probably not possible to have a conscious experience without paying some kind or degree of attention to the stimulus, and it is also doubtful whether what would normally be regarded as a conscious experience is possible without the existence of at least working memory. In order to see how we might deal with this problem, we must briefly consider what is currently known about attention and memory.

Memory

Memory was originally thought to be a single faculty. However most researchers today think of it as a number of systems and subsystems. The classifications used in relation to memory seem to be almost as numerous as the research groups involved, but three stand out.

One of these systems of classification (Kupfermann, 1991) subdivides memory into declarative memory (which does depend on consciousness, can be laid down after a single event and encodes information about auto-biographical events that can be expressed in declarative sentences) and reflexive or procedural memory (which does not depend on conscious processes, builds up slowly over many repetitions and is expressed as improved task performance). Reflexive memory can be demonstrated in animals as uncomplicated as the sea slug. In humans, memories usually begin as declarative memories but may then be transformed by constant repetition into reflexive memories (as for example when a task like driving a car eventually becomes largely automatic and unconscious).

In a second conceptualization, memories are classified according to how long ago they were encoded. They can be iconic (up to about a second after the event) (Breitmeyer & Ganz, 1976), short-term (a limited capacity type that lasts up to a few minutes) or long-term (apparently unlimited capacity, duration up to a life-time) (Kupfermann, 1991).

A third classification system (Tulving & Schacter, 1990) holds that there are three kinds of memory: procedural (which underlies changes in skilled performance), semantic (which has to do with acquisition of factual knowledge in the broadest sense) and episodic (which enables people to remember personally experienced events).

The term working memory fits none of these classification systems exactly. It is term that is often used quite imprecisely, which probably encompasses iconic and short-term memory of the declarative, proce-dural, semantic or episodic types, together with an attentional component (Baddeley, 1992).

Mechanism of memory

The mechanism by which memories are laid down is not clear, despite a monumental and exponentially increasing amount of work on the subject over the past few decades. One of the pioneering speculations on the subject was made by the famous neuroanatomist Ramon y Cajal, who suggested that information could be stored by modifying the connections between communicating nerve cells, in order to form associations (Cajal, 1911). This idea was refined in the late 1940s by Konorski (Konorski, 1948) and Hebb (Hebb, 1949). The latter's formalization of the idea, which is known as the Hebb rule and has achieved almost cult status among neuroscientists, is "When an axon of cell A is near enough to excite cell B and repeatedly and persistently takes part in firing it, some growth process or metabolic change takes place in one or both cells such that A's efficiency, as one of the cells firing B, is increased." The impetus for the current enormous popularity of Hebb's rule was the discovery (Lomo, 1966) of a real life cellular process in the central nervous system that appears to embody the rule perfectly. This process is now generally called long-term potentiation (LTP) of synaptic transmission. LTP was first described in detail in the hippocampus (Bliss & Gardner-Medwin, 1973; Bliss & Lomo, 1973) but it has subsequently been found in every area of the central nervous system in which it has been sought. Its inverse, long-term depression (Pockett & Lippold, 1986) has also turned out to be widespread and is similarly important for neural network models of memory. A further level of complexity has been introduced by the recent discovery that both processes are themselves plastic—that is, neural activity not only produces immediately observable LTP and/or LTD (depending on the pattern of the activity and the synapses which were active), but also changes the ability of a synapse to undergo LTP and LTD in the future (Abraham & Bear, 1996).

Empirical localization of memories

In sea slugs and snails, which are animals simple enough for the entire neural circuitry that mediates certain behaviors to be known in detail, it is likely that potentiation and depression of transmission at various specific synapses is not only necessary but also sufficient to account for simple forms of learning (Alkon, 1983; Kandel, et al., 1983). Basic mechanisms tend to be conserved in evolution, so this, along with a good deal of evidence that manipulating LTP does change learning ability in mammals (Castro, Silbert, McNaughton, & Barnes, 1989; Morris, Anderson, Lynch, & Baudry, 1986) suggests that synapses are indeed the cellular location of the changes causing at least some sorts of learning and memory. However the question of where in the brain memories are encoded by such synaptic changes is a vexed one. Here the possibility that different sorts of memories are encoded in different ways becomes relevant.

The original experiments on the subject of memory location were done by Karl Lashley, who ablated various areas of cortex in experimental animals in a search for the "engram", or site of memory storage (Lashley, 1950). Lashley never found his engram and this failure lead to various models of memory that incorporated an almost mystical property of global storage, such as the holographic ideas of Karl Pribram (Pribram, 1991). However recent single cell experiments in animals and brain imaging studies in humans show that distinct cortical areas are active during the perceptual and the working memory phases of a memory task (Goldman-Rakic, 1997). Specifically, perception is correlated with activation of the sensory area of cortex specific to the sense modality used in the task, plus an area of anterior prefrontal cortex. Working memory (which is defined operationally in this case as the memory used to store information in the delay periods of a delayed matching-to-sample task) is correlated with activity only in a particular area of posterior prefrontal cortex. The fact that this area of posterior prefrontal cortex is actually active during the memory phase of the task suggests that working memory may not be due to long-lasting synaptic changes, but simply to continued neural activation. This idea is supported by the fact that gross disruption of neural activity during electroconvulsive therapy destroys memory for events that immediately precede the treatment but leaves older memories intact. The capacity of working memory seems to be limited to approximately seven separate items of information (Miller, 1956); there is no good neurophysiological explanation for this at present, but the limited size of the cortical area that apparently subserves working memory may be relevant.

Longer term memories probably do involve synaptic modification, in different areas of brain from that involved in working memory. The region that is most implicated in the formation or laying down of long-term memories is the hippocampus. Bilateral loss of hippocampal function in humans causes a severe amnesic syndrome in which working memory is preserved, all varieties of memories that were laid down before hippocampal destruction can still be accessed and new motor skills can still be learned; but no new medium-to-long-term declarative memories can be formed (Milner, Corkin, & Teuber, 1968; Scoville, 1968). This clearly indicates that long-term memories are not stored in the hippocampus, but that some form of processing by the hippocampus is necessary for formation of long-term declarative memories. The detailed explanation of this is completely obscure. What is clear though, is that whatever the role of the hippocampus in the encoding or formation of long-term memories, imaging studies show that long-term memory is stored in a distributed cortical system, in which information about specific features is stored close to the regions of cortex that mediate the perception of these features (Ungerleider, 1995).

Separation of memory processes from consciousness of present objects

The very brief overview above suggests that working memory may well be due to continuing activation of neurons in a specific region of the posterior prefrontal cortex, while long-term declarative memory is encoded by the hippocampus and probably stored all over the brain, in a fashion that closely parallels the distributed representation of perception *per se*.

In order to subtract the contribution of working memory from the electromagnetic pattern correlating with conscious sensory perception, it may be sufficient to subtract the pattern occurring during the delay phase of a delayed matching-to-sample task from the pattern occurring during the initial perceptual phase. This manoeuvre would at least be a good start. In the absence of some strategy like this one, it is inevitable that the processes underlying working memory would to some degree contaminate attempts to elucidate the electromagnetic pattern corresponding to conscious perception *per se.*

With regard to long-term memory, similar subtractive paradigms would be necessary (but in this case probably not sufficient) to isolate the electromagnetic patterns correlating with perception *per se* from those due to involuntary memory formation or recall. For example, comparison of the electromagnetic patterns generated by the brain during direct sensory perception of a particular object and during recall of that object from long-term memory could be a method of removing the effects of recall (although this method would obviously not deal with recall of any other object or thought). Examination of the electromagnetic patterns of a person without a functioning hippocampus would certainly eliminate the effects of long-term memory storage processes.

Attention

As with memory, the mechanism of attention is one of the most studied problems in cognitive neuroscience. However it is probably fair to say that our understanding of attention is even less clear than our understanding of memory. At least we can begin with a relatively clear definition: for convenience we will define as "selective attention" any process, voluntary or involuntary, conscious or unconscious, that shapes the selection of one from two or more competing potentially conscious experiences. The broadness of this definition may admit several mechanisms (see below).

Two main metaphors have been proposed in the search for a model of how the brain achieves the outcome of selective attention. The first is a spotlight or searchlight metaphor—the desired information is illuminated by a spotlight and thus made visible or accessible to consciousness (Crick, 1984; Posner, 1980; Shulman, Remington, & McLean, 1979; Tsal, 1983). The second is a filter metaphor—basically the unwanted information is filtered out (Broadbent, 1958; Cheal, 1997; LaBerge, 1995). Neither metaphor as currently stated directly addresses the question of what decides the aim of the spotlight or the shape of the filter, but since we are for the moment concerned only with simple consciousness, we will continue the robust tradition of glossing over this issue.

Some experimental evidence easily fits into the spotlight metaphor: allocation of attention to a particular location in the visual field improves perception at that location, for example. However because a simple spotlight is sometimes insufficient to explain experimental data, several modifications of this metaphor have evolved. The spotlight has been hypothesized as more like a zoom lens that could vary in diameter (Eriksen & StJames, 1986), or as forming a gradient away from one or more areas of concentration (LaBerge & Brown, 1989). Attention gating is another concept along these lines, defining temporal rather than spatial characteristics of the spotlight (Reeves & Sperling, 1986). A neurophysio-logical mechanism for implementing the spotlight or searchlight has been proposed by Crick (Crick, 1984), who suggests that the expression of the searchlight (or multiple searchlights) may be the production of rapid bursts of firing in a subset of thalamic neurons, which in turn act on selected cortical neurons to facilitate formation of transient "cell assemblies". This speculation has not so far been tested experimentally.

Intuitively appealing as the spotlight metaphor may be, however, (particularly in conjunction with the "theatre" metaphor of consciousness in general (Baars, 1997a)) it has so far failed to vanquish its major competitor, the filter metaphor. The problem is that the two metaphors are difficult to distinguish experimentally. Both of them in effect predict that wanted information should be represented in the brain strongly and unwanted information represented weakly, or not at all.

The filter metaphor proposes that some sort of matched filter is used for rejecting unwanted information (LaBerge, 1995) (and in some versions of the scheme, also for facilitating the entry of desired informa-tion to consciousness(Cheal, 1997)). Any such filter must be an adaptive one, because there must exist a facility for changing it in accordance with an internal template that specifies what is to be attended to. Thus the filter metaphor of attention also intimately involves memory. Each time a stimulus is presented, it must be measured against some sort of neural template, which has to be retrieved from an updatable context system or memory store.

Location of attention systems in the brain

Brain imaging techniques and data from neurological deficits in attention suggest the existence of four differently located neural networks in the brain subserving the *process* of selective attention. It is tempting to speculate that these different attentional networks may implement fundamentally different mechanisms, although there is presently little evidence to support this. The *effects* of these attentional processes are clearly to be found in any brain area that subserves whatever function or percept is the object of selective attention at any given time.

The networks subserving the process of selective attention include:

(a) a posterior parietal system (Belin, et al., 1998; Buchel & Friston, 1997; Buchel, et al., 1998; Buck, Black, Behrmann, Caldwell, & Bronskill, 1997; Carter, Mintun, & Cohen, 1995; Corbetta, et al., 1998; Corbetta & Shulman, 1998; Corbetta, Shulman, Miezin, & Petersen, 1995; Coull & Frith, 1998; Coull & Nobre, 1998; Culham, et al., 1998; Fink, Dolan, Halligan, Marshall, & Frith, 1997; Le, Pardo, & Hu, 1998; Lejeune, et al., 1997; Lumer, Friston, & Rees, 1998; Nagahama, et al., 1998; Nobre, et al., 1997; Pugh, et al., 1996)

(b) an anterior system in the cingulate gyrus (Badgaiyan & Posner, 1998; Benedict, et al., 1998; Carter, Mintun, & Cohen, 1995; Carter, Mintun, Nichols, & Cohen, 1997; Davis, Taylor, Crawley, Wood, & Mikulis, 1997; Jueptner, et al., 1997; Lejeune, et al., 1997; Lockwood, Murphy, & Khalak, 1997; Nobre, et al.,

1997; Tzourio, et al., 1997)(which, however, was specifically observed not to be activated in certain dichotic listening tasks (Pugh, et al., 1996))

(c) a system involving the thalamus (Carter, Mintun, & Cohen, 1995; Frith & Friston, 1996; Lockwood, Murphy, & Khalak, 1997; Mataro, Garcia-Sanchez, Junque, Estevez-Gonzalez, & Pujol, 1997; Portas, et al., 1998)

(d) surprisingly, the cerebellum also appears to be involved, in a way that is independent of task-related motor learning (Akshoomoff, Courchesne, & Townsend, 1997; Allen, Buxton, Wong, & Courchesne, 1997; Le, Pardo, & Hu, 1998; Lejeune, et al., 1997; Rees, Frackowiak, & Frith, 1997).

The cingulate and posterior parietal systems are also sometimes described as involving areas of prefrontal cortex which are concerned with working memory. This suggests either that the task used did not sufficiently distinguish between working memory and attention, or that the filter metaphor (which as already pointed out involves working memory more than does the spotlight metaphor) may be the more relevant to these attentional systems.

It may in fact be the case that the spotlight metaphor applies to the thalamic attention system and the filter metaphor to the cingulate/parietal systems. This idea is given some support by the finding (Portas, et al., 1998) that attention-related thalamic activity is seen more under conditions of low arousal than under conditions of high arousal. This suggests that the main attentional function of thalamocortical loops may be to selectively modulate the excitability of the cortex. Perhaps when cortical neurons are relatively hyperpolarised, the attentional role of the thalamus may be to "spotlight" various general cortical areas in order to bring them closer to the threshold for firing action potentials (see Appendix B), so that finer-tuned, more delicate facilitation provided by the filter-based systems of the cortical attention areas can be effective.

The role of the cerebellum in all this is presently entirely unclear. One group (Akshoomoff, Courchesne, & Townsend, 1997) suggests that the cerebellum is "a master computational system that anticipates and adjusts responsiveness to a variety of brain systems (including attention) to efficiently achieve goals determined by cerebral and other subcortical systems". Who knows.

Whatever the mechanism by which they work, it is clear that the final effect of all of these systems for directing attention is to make one particular feature of the environment "take over" consciousness, at the expense of other features. Imaging studies show that the neural events underlying this take place in whatever area of sensory cortex is dedicated to the particular sense involved: i.e. in auditory cortex for auditory tasks (Belin, et al., 1998; Frith & Friston, 1996; Fujiwara, Nagamine, Imai, Tanaka, & Shibasaki, 1998; Pugh, et al., 1996; Tzourio, et al., 1997), in the visual cortex for visual tasks (Buchel & Friston, 1997; Fink, Dolan, Halligan, Marshall, & Frith, 1997; Haug, Baug, & Paulus, 1998; Hillyard, Vogel, & Luck, 1998; Watanabe, et al., 1998a; Watanabe, et al., 1998b) and in the somatosensory cortex for somatosensory tasks (Mima, Nagamine, Nakamura, & Shibasaki, 1998). The modulation caused by attention seems to be to enhance activity due to the attended inputs and this enhancement is uniformly found to occur in both primary and secondary sensory areas; i.e. in the visual system, as early in the processing chain as V1.

Separation of attentional processes from perception

It should be clear from the above that it is not possible to separate the *effects* of attentional processes from conscious perception *per se*. Conscious perception is only possible when some degree of attention is being paid to the object of perception, and imaging studies show that the effects of the attentional process are inextricably intertwined with the neurophysiology of perception. Whether it is possible in principle to remove the contribution of the *processes* directing attention to the overall electromagnetic pattern correlating with perception is difficult to say. Apparently the contribution of thalamic mechanisms can be removed if the overall level of arousal is already high. Likewise it has been shown that some tasks do not use the cingulate system. Whether perception is possible without activation of the parietal attentional network is doubtful, however.

Summary

In order to establish the fundamental principle about the nature of consciousness that is being proposed here, the first step is to determine whether or not there do exist spatiotemporal electromagnetic patterns that covary with the states and contents of consciousness. This chapter has laid down a fairly demanding set of criteria by which to judge experimental evidence on the issue. In the next four chapters, these criteria are used to examine a number of experiments already described in the scientific literature which may be taken as supporting our fundamental proposal.

CHAPTER TWO: STATES OF CONSCIOUSNESS

- ❖ *Waking and dreaming—Origin and meaning of gamma waves*
- ❖ *Sleep—Light sleep—Deep sleep—Transitions between wakefulness and sleep*
- ❖ *A fourth state of consciousness? Alpha, Mu, Tau and Theta rhythms*
- ❖ *The EEG of drowsiness—The EEG of meditation*

This chapter asks the question "can we tell what state of consciousness a person is in just by examining their EEG?" The answer it comes up with is a slightly qualified "yes".

The three major states of consciousness are usually regarded as being waking, sleeping and dreaming. As it turns out, these states, and various substates of them, are characterised by quite clearcut differences in the pattern of electromagnetic oscillations that can be recorded from the scalp, by either EEG (electroencephalograpy) or MEG (magnetoencephalography). Table 2 shows the various frequencies of oscillation that can be detected in EEG records and their proponderance in various states and substates of consciousness. In general, waking and dreaming are characterised by low-amplitude, relatively high frequency oscillations that are often called "desynchronised" EEG. Non-dreaming sleep involves so-called "synchronised" EEG waves, which are larger and slower.

Table 2: EEG Rhythms

Name	Oscillation frequency (cycles/sec)	Conscious correlates
Fast waves	**Over 8 Hz**	**Waking**
Alpha	8–13 Hz	Relaxed wakefulness, eyes closed
[Kappa]	[8–13 Hz]	[Artefact of eye movements]
Mu (Rolandic)	7–11 Hz arch-shaped waves	Blocked by body movements
Tau	8–10 Hz	Blocked by audition
Beta	13–30 Hz	Wakefulness
Gamma	30–80 Hz (but often referred to simply as 40 Hz)	Active cognition, during either wakefulness, REM sleep or occasionally slow wave sleep
Lambda	Sharp saw-tooth transients	Scanning visual images: rare
Slow waves	**Under 8 Hz**	**Drowsiness and Sleep**
Theta	4–8 Hz	Drowsiness: alpha dropout
Sleep spindles	1–2s bursts of 7–14 Hz, every 5–10s	Mostly Stage 2 sleep
Delta	1–4 Hz	Stage 3 and 4 (deep) sleep: the deeper the sleep, the larger and slower the waves

Waking and Dreaming

Waking and dreaming are obviously different states of consciousness, but they are similar in that subjective sensory and cognitive experiences are a prominent feature of both. Interestingly, the EEG of the two states is indistinguishable, apart from the rapid eye movements that give the dreaming state the label REM sleep. The EEG state which is common to dreaming sleep and waking is often called desynchronised EEG, because it is composed of low amplitude, relatively fast oscillations that have some of the characteristics of 1/f noise. The frequency range of the oscillations is from around 20 to 80 Hz. Such oscillations are now generally termed gamma waves. Sometimes they are referred to under the loose rubric "40Hz", although only some are actually oscillating at exactly 40 Hz.

Two major differences between waking and dreaming are:

(a) In the waking state, sensory input comes from the outside world via the sense organs. In the dream state, the outside world is largely blocked out (although there is some suggestion that auditory input is still possible), with sensory experiences being generated by some kind of intracortical interaction

(b) In the waking state it is relatively easy to form long-term memories of what is experienced, whereas in REM sleep the formation of memories lasting longer than 5 or 10 minutes is rare.

As mentioned, dreaming mostly occurs during an EEG state that is associated with rapid eye movements (REM) but is otherwise indistinguishable from waking EEG. This is inferred because people woken out of a state of REM sleep usually report that they have just been dreaming. Because dreams are rarely reported on awakening from other stages of sleep, it used to be thought that dreaming only occurs in REM sleep. However there is now considerable evidence that dreams can occur during all stages of sleep, including deep, slow-wave sleep (Antrobus, 1983; Cavallero, Cicogna, Natale, Occhionero, & Zito, 1992; Cavallero, Foulkes, Hollifield, & Terry, 1990; Foulkes & Schmidt, 1983). Little work has been done on the EEG concomitants of non-REM (NREM) dreaming, but an attenuated gamma activity can sometimes be seen superimposed on the slow wave EEG (Llinas & Ribary, 1993). It is tempting to suppose that this corresponds to NREM dreaming.

Origin and meaning of gamma waves

Perhaps surprisingly considering the recent flurry of hypotheses about the functions of so-called 40-Hz, or gamma waves, the cellular mechanisms generating them are poorly understood. Direct experimental observation shows that thalamic cells which project to the cortex do oscillate at around 40 Hz, owing both to intrinsic mechanisms due to membrane conductances and extrinsic network mechanisms (Steriade, 1999). For example, cells in the intralaminar nucleus of the thalamus spontaneously discharge 40 Hz bursts of spikes firing at about 1000 Hz, during both waking consciousness and REM sleep (Steriade, Curro Dossi, & Contreras, 1993). Some of these intralaminar cells project, with abnormally high conduction velocities, to the association cortex (Steriade, Dossi, Pare, & Oakson, 1991). In this context it is interesting that the intralaminar nucleus of the thalamus seems to be one of the few structures in the brain which is absolutely necessary for the preservation of waking consciousness (Bogen, 1995a; Bogen, 1995b; Bogen, 1997). This suggests that the intralaminar nucleus of the thalamus might in fact be the pacemaker for cortical 40 Hz oscillations, as the reticular nucleus is for sleep spindles and delta oscillations (see later sections). There is evidence from MEG recordings (Ribary, et al., 1991) that mass oscillations at around 40 Hz sweep in waves across the cortex from front to back (although this evidence is apparently controversial (Hari & Salmelin, 1997)). These studies show a striking coherence between cortical and thalamic sites of origin, which again suggests that the oscillation is a recurrent thalamocortical one.

However, this reasonably good evidence that thalamic input is important in generation of gamma oscillations notwithstanding, several models for strictly cortical generation of gamma waves have been promulgated. Such models differ mainly in whether they see the major factor in the generation of gamma frequency oscillations as being cortical network properties (i.e. local feedback loops) (Bressler & Freeman, 1980; Eeckman & Freeman, 1990; Freeman, 1991b) or the intrinsic oscillatory properties of some cortical cells (Llinas, Grace, & Yarom, 1991), or both (Jefferys, Traub, & Whittington, 1996; Whittington, Traub, & Jefferys, 1995). Each of these purely cortical models is effective in generating gamma oscillations theoretically and it is quite likely that all of them reflect some aspects of the truth, perhaps to differing extents in different regions of the brain. The only mathematical EEG simulation that reproduces gamma band activity (and also the synchrony of oscillations at separate sites that has been measured in the visual system) does include a component for subcortical inputs as well as both local and long-range cortical interactions (Wright, 1997; Wright & Liley, 1995).

In any case, whatever the origin of the 40 Hz oscillations that can be recorded at the scalp, it seems that whenever a human subject reports conscious experience, be this in the context of a dream or of wakefulness, 40 Hz oscillations are present. Conversely it is likely (though not at this stage proven) that whenever 40 Hz oscillations are present there is some degree of conscious experience. This suggests that at the very least, 40 Hz neural oscillations are somehow associated with conscious experience.

Sleep

The major biologically important difference between the states of waking and sleep is that in sleep, external sensory stimuli are prevented from affecting the cerebral cortex and thus from entering consciousness. The mechanisms by which this block is imposed are known in some detail.

The brain region involved is the thalamus. The thalamus is perfectly placed for the role of regulating access of sensory stimuli to the cortex, because it is the one structure through which the neural pathways of all sensory systems (except the olfactory system) must pass on their way to the cortex. Not only are sensory messages not transmitted through the thalamus in sleep, but the state of the thalamus that blocks sensory traffic also causes major slow rhythmic activity in the cortex, of a sort which would overwhelm any of the smaller, faster and more complex sensory EEG patterns which did escape thalamic blockade.

The cellular mechanisms by which the thalamus either transmits sensory information or puts the cortex into a sleeping state are remarkably well worked out, but quite complex. Readers not particularly interested in neurophysiology could profitably skip the next few sections without losing too much of the plot.

> Thalamic neurons have two distinct modes of firing, depending on their resting membrane potential (Steriade & Llinas, 1988). During the waking state, they are relatively depolarized. In this condition they can be influenced by synaptic input from the

peripheral sense organs to fire long trains of action potentials, which more or less faithfully transmit sensory information to the cortex (with some modification by attentional systems). During EEG-synchronised sleep, thalamic cells are basically more hyperpolarized. In this state they fire continuously in rhythmic bursts, for reasons which are described in the following sections. The blockade of incoming stimulus traffic from the periphery during this bursting mode is due to the fact that the neurons alternate between (a) being so hyperpolarized that incoming synaptic traffic does not bring the membrane potential close enough to threshold to cause action potentials, and (b) firing rebound bursts of action potentials after the cyclic periods of hyperpolarization (which also has the effect of blocking information that might otherwise be conveyed by patterned firing due to input from the sense organs).

The cellular mechanisms in the thalamus that underlie the states of light sleep and deep sleep are as follows.

Light Sleep

The onset of sleep is signalled by sleep spindles. These are 1–2 second sequences of 7–14 Hz waves that wax and wane in amplitude so that each sequence has the shape of a spindle. A spindle occurs every 5 or 10 seconds during this stage of sleep.

Sleep spindles are generated by the reticular nucleus of the thalamus (Steriade, 1994). The reticular nucleus is a thin sheet of GABAergic inhibitory cells covering three sides of the thalamus. There are reciprocal synaptic connections between the reticular nucleus and each of the various other nuclei in the body of the dorsal thalamus. The nuclei within the body of the thalamus also send thalamocortical axons to various specific areas of cortex and receive corticothalamic connections back from the same areas of cortex to which they send axons.

The evidence that the reticular nucleus is the pacemaker of thalamic spindle oscillations (Steriade, 1999) is convincing. During spindling, reticular neurons show a slowly growing and decaying depolarization with superimposed spike barrages at a frequency of 7–14 Hz. This bursting pattern of firing is generated intrinsically, by interaction of the properties of six different types of ion channels in the cell membranes of the reticular cells. Reticular neurons are GABAergic inhibitory neurons, so the 7–14 Hz spike barrages they produce cause bursts of IPSPs in the cells to which they project in the main body of the thalamus. The successive IPSPs in each burst summate until they make the thalamic cell internally negative enough to activate an unusual type of calcium channel, which has the property that it is inactivated at rest and de-inactivated by hyperpolarization. When this calcium channel has been de-inactivated, the return to a more positive membrane potential after the spindle burst of IPSPs (which return is, incidentally, speeded up by the presence of an equally unusual non-inactivating sodium channel) can now open the calcium channels to generate a calcium spike. The calcium spike in turn triggers a so-called rebound burst of high frequency (200–400Hz) normal sodium action potentials in the thalamocortical cells. This burst of spikes is transferred to the cortex and it, together with its synaptic effects, show up on EEG records as sleep spindles. Complex, but effective!

The visibility of spindles in the EEG is assisted by the fact that sleep spindles in quite large areas of the cortex tend to be synchronised. This is because the bursts of IPSPs in the thalamic cells are synchronised, which in turn is because the pacemaking bursts in the reticular neurons are synchronised. Synchronisation of bursts in the reticular neurons may be because these are all interconnected within the reticular nucleus, by both dendro-dendritic synapses and gap junctions. Synchronisation may also be assisted by electric field-based volume conduction effects.

Deep Sleep

Spindling can be transmuted into the slower, continuous delta waves of deep sleep by a progressive hyperpolarization of the thalamic neurons. This is generated as sleep deepens because of a progressive decrease in firing rates of the cortical neurons that project excitatory synapses back to the thalamus. At a thalamic membrane potential more negative than around -70 mV, a non-specific cation channel called I_h is activated and the interaction between this current and the transient calcium current (I_t) referred to above in relation to the spindling sequence gives rise to the larger, slower oscillation of membrane potential that characterises delta sleep. In very deep sleep, the 1–4 Hz rhythm of delta sleep is further sculpted by an even slower rhythm with a period of between 2 and 10 seconds. This slow rhythm is disrupted by ketamine and thus probably involves NMDA receptor-mediated excitatory synaptic transmission, in some way that is not yet understood.

Transitions between synchronised and non-synchronised EEG

The above factors explain at a cellular level the generation of the various EEG rhythms of EEG-synchronised sleep. However they do not explain what leads the brain into a sleeping state in the first place, or what pitches it from the state of EEG synchronised sleep into the states of waking or REM sleep.

The main neuronal site involved in waking the brain up seems to be a small territory in the midbrain, at the mesopontine junction. Two groups of cholinergic cells in this region, plus the norepinephrine-containing cells of the locus coeruleus and the serotonin (5-HT)-containing cells of the dorsal raphe nucleus (all in the same restricted area) act conjointly on thalamic and cortical cells during wakefulness. In REM sleep, only the cholinergic neurons are involved and the locus coeruleus and raphe nucleus are virtually silent. This group of brain regions is sometimes called the ascending reticular activating system. The cellular mechanisms by which these activating neurons act are:

(a)   cholinergic neurons hyperpolarize the cells of the thalamic reticular nucleus by increasing a potassium conductance in those cells, thus cutting off the depolarizing envelope of the spindle oscillations. Norepinephrine and 5-HT also hyperpolarize the cells of the reticular nucleus into the tonically firing range of wakefulness.

(b)   these transmitters also depolarize the cells in the main body of the thalamus, bringing them out of the range where delta oscillations are generated.

What activates the midbrain nuclei in question is controversial. One biological clock for the sleep-wake cycle is located in the suprachiasmatic nucleus of the hypothalamus, which has a direct link to the eyes (Kandel, Schwartz, & Jessell, 1991). As in the thalamic reticular nucleus, the cells of the suprachiasmatic nucleus are linked together by dendrodendritic synapses, which predisposes them to synchronous activity. This nucleus is spontaneously active and inactive in a circadian rhythm, which is entrained to the light-dark cycle in the environment by the retino-hypothalamic pathway. Whether this affects the thalamic reticular nucleus directly or through the ascending reticular activating system in the brainstem is unclear.

A fourth state of consciousness?

The three accepted states of consciousness are, as discussed above, waking, dreaming and sleeping. However, there is some basis for proposing the existence of a fourth state of consciousness, distinct from the other three. Whether this condition is in fact conceived as a distinct state unto itself, or as the basal state of waking consciousness, or simply as a transition state between waking and sleep, is a moot and probably not terribly important point. Whichever name you choose, this state is interesting from the point of view of understanding the varieties of consciousness.

By and large, the Western intellectual tradition emphasizes intentionality as a defining feature of consciousness (Rao, 1998). This means that waking consciousness is widely held to be necessarily *of* or *about* something. Such a view has been emphasized by Bretano, Husserl, Freud and Satre, it is the basis of phenomenology and it is espoused to some degree by most contemporary Western philosophers e.g. Searle (1983). However the Eastern perspective on consciousness is quite different. Indian philosophy sees consciousness as basically non-intentional. Pure consciousness, or waking consciousness which is not *of* anything, is widely regarded as being not only theoretically possible, but attainable by ordinary persons. Indeed, various practical systems of meditation which have the immediate object of allowing this state to be reached by individuals on a regular basis have been taught for many centuries by Hindu and Buddhist masters in India, China and Japan.

EEG measurements tend to support the Eastern rather than the Western view on this issue. There are a number of distinct EEG conditions associated with what is subjectively reported to be a non-intentional state of consciousness, accessible by meditation or various other simple strategies. First the relevant EEG oscillations and their likely origins will be described and then the association between these EEG features and the subjectively reported state.

Alpha rhythm

When a healthy adult human in a relaxed frame of mind rests with closed eyes, rhythmic activity with a frequency between 8 and 13 Hz can often be recorded from the posterior regions of the scalp, over the visual cortex. This so-called alpha rhythm can be plainly seen in raw EEG records and was first described 70 years ago by Hans Berger (Berger, 1929). Because it is normally blocked by opening the eyes and strongly suppressed during visual stimuli, visual memory tasks and visual imagery

(Kaufman, Schwarz, Salustri, & Williamson, 1990; Michel, Kaufman, & Williamson, 1994; Salenius, Kajola, Thompson, Kosslyn, & Hari, 1995), alpha rhythm is generally considered to be the idling rhythm of the visual system. Consideration of whether or not this is true should probably be deferred until after the section on generation of the alpha rhythm, below.

Despite a large amount of work on the subject in the 70 years since human alpha was first described, the mechanism by which this major brain rhythm is generated is still controversial. Several hypotheses will be considered here. We might as well start with the most controversial one.

1.   This is that the alpha rhythm is not generated by the brain at all, but by the corneoretinal potential, as modulated by 10 Hz physiological tremor in the eye muscles (Ennever, Lippold, & Novotny, 1971; Lippold, 1970a; Lippold, 1970b; Lippold, 1970c; Lippold, 1971; Lippold, 1973; Lippold & Novotny, 1970).

The idea that the alpha rhythm is essentially an artefact has always been in the back of physiologists' minds and in fact worried Berger, the discoverer of human EEG, so much that he delayed publication of his findings for some time while he tried to convince himself that this was not the case. Today this hypothesis remains so threatening to EEG afficionados that most writers on electroencephalography either ignore it completely, or mention it briefly only to dismiss it without further consideration. In fact the idea, at least in the form outlined above, is supported by several experimental observations which can not be easily explained on the usual assumption that alpha rhythm is produced by the cerebral cortex under the recording electrode, and in my opinion it must be taken very seriously indeed. Observations supporting the hypothesis are as follows.

First, alpha rhythm is still present over an empty cranium after either total cerebral hemispherectomy (Cobb & Sears, 1960; Marshall & Walker, 1950; Obrador & Larramendi, 1950), or occipital lobectomy (Masland, Austin, & Grant, 1949). While it is conceivable that this simply results from far-field recording of sources in the intact cerebrum on the other side of the brain, it is difficult to reconcile this explanation with the observation that in some cases alpha rhythm over the section of empty skull was actually larger than that over the side with intact brain under it.

Secondly, it can be shown that in normal subjects tremor of the extraocular muscles is indeed related to alpha activity, as follows:

(a) Physiological tremor occurs in all voluntary muscles as a natural part of the servo-mechanism controlling muscle length. It results from oscillation in the neural feedback loop between muscle and spinal cord—the stretch reflex arc. Normal electro-oculograms recorded between the inner and outer canthus of the eye or from sites above and below the eye do show a fine 10 Hz tremor. A roughly 10 Hz in-out mechanical oscillation of the eye can also be shown to take place. There is good correspondence between these two 10 Hz oscillations and alpha as recorded over the occipital part of the skull.

(b) At normal temperatures, physiological muscle tremor has a frequency of about 10 Hz, but when the muscle is cooled, the properties of the feedback loop are modified and the frequency of the tremor slows down. When right or left eye sockets are cooled or warmed individually in a subject who normally shows a standard 10Hz alpha rhythm, the frequency of the alpha slows or increases as predicted by the hypothesis, *only on the side of the head corresponding to the cooled or warmed eye.* Thus if the right eye is cooled to 5°C and the left eye warmed to 45°C, the alpha rhythm as recorded at the back of the head slows down on the right side and speeds up on the left. This is not explainable by any action of temperature on the visual cortex via the optic nerve, because the optic nerve largely transmits to the opposite visual cortex.

(c) Another way of modifying the loop properties in a servo-mechanism is to introduce a step function into the loop. If the loop gain is high enough, this produces a damped oscillation, time-locked to the stimulus. If a step function is introduced into the feedback loop involving the extraocular muscles by simply prodding the eyeball, alpha waves become phase-locked to the prod.

(d) About 11% of people do not show any alpha rhythm at all. There is no evidence that these people are in any way lacking in visual consciousness and indeed some evidence that their eye-sight is abnormally good and that they do not have the normal eye-muscle tremor. If the eye muscles of such subjects are experimentally fatigued in various ways, both muscle tremor and alpha rhythm develop.

(e) The amount of alpha can be shown to depend on eye position. If forced upward movements of the open eyes are made, tremor and alpha both appear.

(f) It is well known that occipital alpha is usually present only when the eyes are closed and that it is blocked by opening the eyes, or by visual imagery. This may be because eye fixation caused by the visual cortex during the perception of a visual image prevents tremor. Eye fixation normally occurs in order to maintain a stable image on the retina. Alpha can be obtained with eyes open; most easily by placing an opaque screen in front of the eyes so as to prevent any images falling on the retina, or with considerably more difficulty by gazing fixedly for a very long time at an unchanging scene, which results in fading of the stabilised retinal image.

Thirdly, the corneoretinal potential (CRP) does seem to vary in concert with alpha amplitude. The corneoretinal potential is quite a large potential (about 80 mV) which can be recorded between the cornea and the back of the eye. It is usually measured by recording its movements, using the electro-oculogram. The CRP increases in the light and decreases in the dark, so it is considered that its cause is most likely the metabolism of visual purple. In light conditions, when the CRP is relatively large, alpha waves are also large. When the CRP is reduced by darkness, so is alpha amplitude.

Despite the rather compelling nature of the above arguments, however, it should be pointed out that even if the main generator of the alpha rhythm were to be accepted as being the corneoretinal potential, such large electromagnetic oscillations across the cortex would be very likely to induce currents and action potential firing in cortical cells anyway (see Chapter 7). Therefore the immediate cause of at least some of the alpha frequency oscillation normally measured over the occipital scalp is still likely to be brain activity at around 10 Hz.

2.   The second hypothesis is that alpha rhythm in the cortex is generated by pacemakers in the thalamus. This idea too is somewhat controversial. Because sleep spindles have a frequency in the alpha range, experimental observations on the thalamic site of generation of spindles in barbiturate-anesthetised cats (Andersen & Andersson, 1968) were initially treated as revealing the mechanism of alpha rhythm generation. However, one major contributor to the field (Steriade & Llinas, 1988) argues that there are a number of differences between alpha and spindles: (a) their topography is different, with alpha-type rhythms being recorded from posterior areas around the occipital cortex and posterior temporal areas and spindles mostly from anterior areas (b) their structure is different, with alpha waves occurring in very long trains, while spindles are grouped in short sequences that recur periodically and in which the amplitude of the waves increases and then decreases in the shape of a spindle and the frequency decreases as amplitude increases, and (c) their behavioral concomitants are different, with spindling occurring during unconsciousness and being associated with depressed synaptic transmission through the thalamus, while alpha waves occur in the waking state and may increase in prevalence and amplitude during attentional demands. Thus alpha and spindling are now often considered to be quite different oscillations. My personal observations are that alpha spindles can certainly be observed in the

EEG of humans who have their eyes closed but are obviously awake, so the situation seems to me to be less than clearcut at the moment.

In any case, the observable cellular mechanisms that presumably underlie alpha-frequency spindling in some way are outlined above, in the section on light sleep. It is probably fair to say that most neurophysiologists would take these findings as being all that is needed to explain the genesis of alpha-frequency spindles in the EEG.

3.   Another class of ideas on this subject is represented by various mathematical models of the generation of the alpha and other EEG rhythms. These start by making fundamental assumptions about what neuronal groupings and interactions are important in rhythm generation. They then set up a simplified mathematical model of how these elements behave, assigning numerical values to the relevant parameters. In some cases the numerical values are drawn from anatomical and physiological measurements, but in other cases it must be admitted that they are essentially fudge factors, specified simply to make the model's predictions come out as desired. Finally, the models mathematically manipulate these parameters according to specified rules, in order to generate an oscillation in the system which is more or less close in frequency and behavior to the oscillation measured empirically in the brain. If they are useful, such models make specific, experimentally testable predictions about the characteristics of the rhythm whose generation they purport to explain.

There exist two well-developed mathematical models which deal specifically with the genesis of the alpha rhythm. The earlier of the two is that of van Rotterdam and Lopes da Silva (Rotterdam, Silva, Ende, Viergever, & Hermans, 1982; Silva, Hoeks, Smits, & Zetterberg, 1974; Silva, Vos, Mooibroek, & Rotterdam, 1980; Steriade, Gloor, Llinas, Lopes de Silva, & Mesulam, 1990). This model proceeds from the assumption that the alpha rhythm is generated partly by thalamic driving of cortical cells (as outlined in the section on the cellular mechanisms of spindling) and partly by intracortical processes. Because measured intracortical correlations or coherences in the alpha range are reported by this group to be larger than thalamocortical coherences, the model is biased towards intracortical generation of alpha. The model can be regarded as primarily a local model, in that it assumes only an infinite one-dimensional chain of pyramidal cells and interneurons, interconnected by collaterals and inhibitory fibers. When the neuronal chain is driven by a spatially and temporally noisy signal (from the thalamus), dispersive waves propagate along it at the frequency of the alpha rhythm. Anatomically derived size parameters are used and the wave consequently moves at approximately the speed that can be measured for the alpha rhythm. In other words, the model achieves a good fit with the temporal and spatial properties of the alpha rhythm at a millimetric scale. However this is at the price of linearising the system, imposing a grossly simplified anatomical structure and introducing a strength of coupling which is arbitrarily defined. Boundary conditions are open and waves outside the alpha range are not considered explicitly (Wright & Kydd, 1992).

The second mathematical model dealing specifically with the origin of the alpha rhythm is that of Nunez (Nunez, 1995). This model involves a local component but also brings global considerations into the picture, in the form of an influence from cortico-cortical association fibers. The model consists of two linear integral equations for global dynamics (representing the times taken for neural impulses to propagate in cortico-cortical association fibers) coupled to a third, generally nonlinear equation for local dynamics (which depends on the rise and decay times of cortical postsynaptic potentials). The model also introduces boundary conditions imposed by the skull, which leads to the prediction that alpha is actually a global standing wave. Usefully, this model makes two critical and falsifiable predictions—one of which has been criticized and the other falsified. It predicts (a) a negative correlation between brain size and fundamental mode alpha frequency and (b) a positive correlation between cortico-cortical long range fiber conduction velocity and fundamental mode alpha frequency. Evidence cited by the model's author in favor of the first of these predictions is attacked and the second prediction is experimentally falsified by Sergejew (Sergejew, 1997). Probably the main theoretical weakness of the model is that it fails to give subcortical (i.e. thalamic) influences any consideration at all, thus ignoring a large body of empirical data which says that they probably are important. Again, as with the Amsterdam model, the genesis of EEG oscillations with dominant frequencies other than that of the alpha rhythm is not dealt with.

A third mathematical model which generates alpha-frequency oscillations, along with all the other major cerebral rhythms, is that of Wright and Liley (Wright & Liley, 1995). This model has been discussed already in the section on the generation of gamma rhythms. It provides a useful bridge between the microscopic and the macroscopic scales in the understanding of EEG rhythms.

4.   Current dogma among magnetoencephalographers is that alpha is generated in the visual cortex, mainly in the region of the calcarine sulcus (Chapman, Ilmoniemi, Barbanera, & Romani, 1984) and around the parieto-occipital sulcus (Salmelin & Hari, 1994a; Vvedensky, Ilmoniemi, & Kajola, 1986). These conclusions are based on calculations of the site of hypothetical dipole sources which best explain the observed scalp recordings (proceeding from the assumption that the generator of alpha is somewhere in the cerebral cortex).

In summary, it can be postulated that one's views of the origin of the alpha rhythm are likely to be colored by one's professional background. More usefully, it can also be stated with some confidence that the labeling of all EEG oscillations that have a dominant mode in the frequency range

8–13 Hz as "alpha" is likely to be a gross oversimplification. There are probably a number of different "alpha" rhythms.

Mu rhythm

One form of spontaneous EEG activity in the frequency range 8–13 Hz is called the mu rhythm (Gastaut, 1952; Kuhlman, 1978). This can be recorded over the motor cortex near the top of the head. Its earlier name was the Rolandic rhythm. It is considered by magnetoencephalographers to be generated near the primary somatosensory hand projection cortex (Tiihonen, M.Kajola, & Hari, 1989) and is blocked by body movements and by tactile stimuli. The rhythm consists of two main frequency components, one around 10 Hz and the other around 20 Hz (but usually not exactly harmonic frequencies). The source locations of these as determined by MEG are usually about 5 mm more anterior for the 20 Hz than the 10 Hz rhythms (Salmelin & Hari, 1994b). Human rolandic MEG activity has a close temporal relationship to peripheral muscular activity (Conway, et al., 1995; Salenius, Portin, Kajola, Salmelin, & Hari, 1997; Salenius, Salmelin, Neuper, Pfurtscheller, & Hari, 1996; Volkmann, et al., 1996) and there is some suggestion that the 20 Hz rhythm is predominantly related to the generation of motor activity while the 10 Hz rhythm is related to somatosensation.

Tau rhythm

Yet another 8–10 Hz rhythm is observable over the auditory cortex (Tiihonen, et al., 1991). This one is called the tau rhythm, because it is seen over the temporal lobe. It is dampened by sound stimuli, but not by opening the eyes or by movement. The rhythm has a similar spatial distribution to the auditory evoked magnetic field, with MEG-derived sources in the supratemporal auditory cortex.

Theta Rhythm

The name theta is generally given to EEG oscillations in the frequency range between 4 and 8 Hz. However it is possible that as with the "alpha" rhythm, there is more than one functional rhythm underlying this general class. In fact there are at least three behavioral concomitants of oscillations in the theta frequency range that appear, at first sight anyway, to be quite different, and there are also at least two different sites of origin of such rhythms in the brain.

First, an EEG oscillation around 5–7 Hz occurs in some but not all subjects during the state of drowsiness between the restful alertness of the alpha range and sleep. Secondly, during mental calculation and intensive thinking, one 5–7 Hz MEG signal has been recorded from the frontal cortex (Sasaki, Tsujimoto, Nambu, Matsuzaki, & Kyuhou, 1994) and another from the hippocampus (Tesche, et al., 1995). The genesis of hippocampal theta has been intensively studied in rodents because of its importance in memory formation, but its cellular mechanisms are not yet clear (Stewart & Fox, 1990). Rhythmical EEG activity in the 6–7 Hz range over the frontal midline region has also been correlated with mental activity such as problem solving (Brazier & Casby, 1952; Ishihara & Yoshii, 1972; Mizuki, 1982; Mizuki, 1987; Mizuki, Takii, Nishijima, & Inanaga, 1983; Mizuki, Tanaka, Isozaki, Nishijima, & Inanaga, 1980). Some studies have reported being unable to induce the latter EEG rhythm (Niedermeyer, Krauss, & Peyser, 1989), but this finding was clarified by the observation (Takahashi, Shinomiya, Mori, & Tachibana, 1997) that individuals with frontal midline 6–7 Hz activity during drowsiness also had the same type of activity during mental tasks. It is a reasonable hypothesis that the mental tasks used in the studies showing theta rhythm during intensive thinking may have become either so boring or so fatiguing that they induced a state of drowsiness, so that the two frontal theta rhythms (which apparently have entirely different behavioral correlates) are actually one and the same.

A third, distinctly different kind of mental state underlies the so-called hedonic theta rhythm, which has been observed in young children during very pleasurable activities (Kugler & Laub, 1971; Maulsby, 1971). The response consisted of very strong 4 Hz activity in posterior and central areas, which was different from the 5–6 Hz rhythm produced in drowsiness by the same children. Such rhythms have not been seen in adults during sexual activity (Graber, Rohrbaugh, Newlin, Varner, & Ellingson, 1985), but little else has been done on the EEG correlates of pure pleasure. This seems strange, since one would think that pleasure should be a passingly enjoyable topic to study. Perhaps the Puritan work ethic so necessary for surviving the rigors of a scientific apprenticeship overwhelms such considerations. Or perhaps the problem is simply that granting agencies fail to see the benefits of a scientific understanding of happiness (which, if so, would seem to be remarkably short-sighted in view of the fact that clinical depression is one of the major psychiatric problems of our age).

The EEG of Drowsiness

The EEG of drowsiness will be discussed at this point because some authors consider that the meditational state is simply a finely-held state of drowsiness. The evidence given here suggests that this is not the case.

Drowsiness is hard to define exactly, but in general terms it is the state that normally occurs between waking and sleeping. Frequently drowsiness is defined in terms of a decrease, intermittency and finally cessation of the alpha rhythm. However about 11% of normal adults do not show alpha rhythms at all and most of those who do neither look nor report feeling drowsy up to 20 seconds after alpha dropout (Santamaria & Chiappa, 1987). Furthermore, there is considerable EEG variability in individual transitions from waking to sleep, both between subjects and between consecutive episodes of drowsiness in the same subject. All that being said, it is possible to make some generalizations about the EEG of drowsiness (although no mechanisms can be deduced from these, because of the frequent exceptions to them).

First, awake alpha is usually seen over the occipital lobes. During drowsiness, this tends to disappear and be replaced by temporal (10% of subjects) and/or centro-frontal (75% of subjects) "alpha" (Santamaria & Chiappa, 1987). As mentioned earlier, what is described as temporal alpha is probably actually the tau rhythm. If frontal alpha is in fact generated in the frontal lobes it may be associated with disappearance of thoughts, as occipital alpha is associated with disappearance of visual sensations and tau with disappearance of auditory sensations. Centrofrontal alpha appears in some drowsy subjects both when using a non-cephalic reference (balanced neck/chest) and with longitudinal bipolar montages, so it is not an artefact of false extension by the ear reference of posterior alpha to the anterior leads. Also, the centrofrontal alpha usually has a slightly slower frequency than the posterior alpha and there is usually a decrease in amplitude of the posterior alpha as frontal alpha appears.

Secondly, the amplitude of the posterior alpha can either decrease smoothly with only minimal slowing during the onset of drowsiness (about 30% of subjects) or it can actually increase, without spreading to the vertex (25% of subjects). One review considers an increase in alpha amplitude and a mild slowing to be the first EEG signs of drowsiness (Erwin, Somerville, & Radtke, 1984).

Thirdly, it is a general statement that slow EEG rhythms increase as drowsiness progresses, but the patterns with which this happens vary. One pattern shows posterior alpha decreasing in amplitude and regularity and becoming intermixed with irregular, moderate amplitude theta/delta oscillations. Sometimes in this pattern the theta and delta activity is present centrofrontally as well. A second pattern, which is very common, consists of runs of centrofrontal, moderate amplitude 3–5 Hz activity concurrent with awake posterior alpha. Various other patterns of slowing or disappearance of alpha and appearance of theta rhythms have also been reported. As well as biological variability, the particular electrode montage used is important in determining which rhythms are seen and which are not. Whatever the cause, the general picture is of a very non-homogeneous transition from waking to sleep EEGs.

The EEG of Meditation

The EEG of meditation, on the other hand, presents a much more homogeneous picture than that of "natural" drowsiness.

The two main meditation traditions which have participated in EEG studies to date are Zen Buddhism and Transcendental Meditation™ (a.k.a TM), a Vedic Hindu-based meditation technique popularized and essentially franchised in the West by Maharishi Mahesh Yogi. There are, of course, many other meditation techniques, but EEG recordings have been done mainly on Zen and TM practitioners. The meditation techniques used by these two traditions have a similar goal. This is a state which is variously described as very restful, silent, often blissful, in which the subject is awake (in fact often feels a heightened alertness), but has no thoughts or sensations, except sometimes a pervading feeling of objectless bliss or ecstasy. These subjective descriptions already differentiate the state from drowsiness.

The techniques used in Zen and TM are in some ways similar, but in other ways distinctly different. Zen meditation involves concentration on some object such as a single thought or sensation, the subject's breathing, or various purposely paradoxical, counterconceptual problems called koans. Beginners usually find difficulty in maintaining concentration. Then, as the subject's ability to concentrate improves, various odd bodily sensations may occur. With perseverance, extraneous thoughts and sensations become less intrusive and fade away completely. Eventually even the object of concentration fades away and a wakeful state variously called "nirvana" or "satori" is achieved. Zazen, the most usual, sitting form of Zen meditation, emphasizes absolute physical stillness in a particular posture during meditations. Sleep and intruding thoughts are positively rejected. The practice is done with the eyes open. There are various sects of Zen Buddhism, and even within one sect the details of meditative procedures depend on the particular Zen master and his estimate of the individual student. A flash of satori can occasionally be achieved instantaneously, given the right mental and physical preparation and a talented teacher, but it is accepted that generally many years of dedicated practice of the technique may be necessary before the desired state can be reached reliably.

In contrast, the technique of TM produces reports of some subjects' achieving the desired state of nothingness after only a few days of practice. TM involves silent mental repetition of a word called a mantra. The main feature of the technique is supposed to be its effortlessness. Neither sleep nor thoughts are rigidly rejected, physical stillness is not particularly emphasized (although it does occur spontaneously, right down to a dramatic slowing of breathing) and the technique is done in any comfortable upright sitting position, with the eyes closed. The immediate aim is a state where spontaneous thoughts cease and finally even the mantra disappears and one is left with a non-intentional state of consciousness called "samadhi" or "pure consciousness". This has been characterised on the basis of physiological measurements as a wakeful, hypometabolic integrated response (Jevning, Wallace, & Beidebach, 1992). Thereafter, repeated experience of this state is said to produce a variety of permanent "higher" states of consciousness. Unlike Zen, the TM system has notably emphasized standardization of teaching methods, which makes it a particularly attractive candidate for scientific study.

The EEG concomitants of meditation in both traditions are similar. The largest study of the EEG of Zen meditation so far has been done by Tomio Hirai (Hirai, 1974), who studied 48 monks of the Soto and Rinzai sects. The meditation experience of these subjects ranged from 22 to 55 years. A good correlation was seen between an independent assessment by the Zen masters of individuals' advancement in the Zen sense and the EEG changes occurring during meditation. The basic EEG correlate of meditations that were deemed to be successful was the appearance of alpha rhythm in the eyes-open state (although it should be noted that the monks in the photographs shown by Hirai appear to have their eyes about half closed, as a result of looking downwards at a point about a meter in front of them). The alpha oscillations were more prominent in frontal, central and parietal recording sites than occipital. In those monks with relatively more years of meditation experience the alpha oscillations became larger and slower, particularly at more frontal sites, as a particular meditation progressed in time. In a few of the most advanced monks, high voltage rhythmical theta waves then appeared at all recording sites. These theta waves had characteristics different from the theta waves seen in drowsiness. They tended to be of higher amplitude than the low-voltage drowsiness theta. Furthermore, in the drowsy state an audible click will stop theta activity and elicit alpha instead. However a click presented during meditative theta elicited a blocking response but no alpha—the EEG was simply desynchronised briefly by the click and the theta rhythm reappeared after 2–3 seconds. Drowsy-type theta was sometimes seen in younger monks during meditation, but this was clearly distinguishable from the theta seen in deep meditation by the advanced monks, both electrophysiologically and by introspective report. Breathing slows down considerably during the meditations of experienced Zen practitioners, but this is a voluntary rather than an involuntary effect, in that the training emphasizes breathing softly and concentrating on breaths.

TM produces a remarkably similar EEG profile to Zen meditation. Overall, about 40% of meditation time is spent in sleep as defined by the standard EEG sleep criteria. This almost certainly depends simply on how sleep-deprived the particular individual is at the time of meditation. In meditations where sleep does not intervene, the general pattern with TM is that alpha rhythm increases in amplitude, slows down in frequency and extends to anterior channels at the start of the meditation (Banquet, 1973; Wallace, 1970). No obvious correlations are reported between this period and any particular subjective experience. In a second stage, bursts of theta frequencies, different from those of sleep, diffuse from frontal to posterior channels. Periods of theta correspond closely with periods of involuntary breath suspension for up to a minute (NB:TM does not involve any active breath control, or indeed any attention to the breathing at all). During these periods the subjective experience is uniformly reported as peaceful, comfortable or pleasant, with no thoughts but a full, "expanded" awareness of perfect stillness (Farrow & Hebert, 1982; Hebert & Lehman, 1977). This experience is identified by the TM culture as pure consciousness, or transcendence. The end of such periods is signalled by a burst of beta frequency EEG activity and resumption of normal breathing. Particularly during the first part of the pure consciousness periods, coherence between the EEG recorded at different electrode sites, particularly in the theta band, is reported to be very high. However a sharp rise in basal skin resistance is also reported to occur at these times and this together with reference electrode effects might well result in some artefact with regard to coherence measurements.

Thus overall, with two different techniques of meditation, we find that the desired effect of a state of pleasant or even blissful thought-free, non-intentional consciousness, is correlated with the presence of a distinct type of theta frequency EEG activity. It is tempting to identify this with the hedonic theta seen in children, but more work is necessary in this area before any conclusions can be drawn. The major difference between TM and Zen techniques is that this state seems to be considerably easier to achieve with TM than with Zen meditation.

Since the state is relatively easy to achieve during TM meditations, it is regarded in the TM culture as merely the baseline for the development of three permanent "higher" states of consciousness. This is in sharp contrast to the situation with most other schools of meditation, where the experience of samadhi or satori (a.k.a. pure consciousness) is regarded as the ultimate goal, to be reached by only a few of those who devote their lives to meditative practices. The Vedic tradition underlying TM says that with repeated meditation practice, the first of three higher states can be stabilized, in which pure consciousness is spontaneously experienced continuously, not only during meditations but during waking, dreaming and even deep sleep. The term "witnessing" is used to describe this state because transcendental consciousness is experienced to be a non-changing level of awareness that serves as a peaceful inner observer or "silent witness" to the active changing states of waking, dreaming and sleep. Witnessing during sleep apparently has some similarities to lucid dreaming, which is a condition in which one is aware that one is dreaming and can control the dream

(LaBerge, 1985). However in the case of witnessing during dreaming, the inner observer takes no part in the dream but simply calmly looks on, as it does also during deep sleep. Remarkably, TM practitioners who report clear experiences of witnessing in sleep do show 6–10 Hz theta-alpha activity simultaneously with delta activity and decreased chin muscle activity during deep sleep (Mason, et al., 1997). Control subjects did not show such EEG activity.

The relationship of meditative theta activity to the theta activity seen in concentration on mental tasks is unclear, but on the face of it, these studies on meditation do seem to provide both objective and subjective evidence for the existence of a fourth state of consciousness, which correlates with the presence of EEG oscillations in the theta-alpha range.

Summary

The experimental work cited in this chapter shows that the existence of the three usually recognized states of consciousness—waking, dreaming and deep sleep—can be accounted for or explained in terms of the hypothesis put forward here. That is, there is good correlation between the presence of certain global electromagnetic oscillations in the brain and the presence of associated states of consciousness.

Specifically, the available evidence supports the postulate that gamma frequency oscillations (20–80 Hz) are the carrier wave of the various modalities of waking and dreaming consciousness (such as olfactory, auditory and visual conscious experience). The conscious contents of these modalities are very likely to be 3–dimensional spatial modulations of the carrier waves, as will be described in later chapters. Deep sleep is associated with electromagnetic oscillations in the frequency range 1–4 Hz and lighter sleep with slightly higher frequency oscillations. There is some evidence suggestive of the existence of a fourth state of consciousness, which may be described as pure, or non-intentional consciousness. This may possibly be identified with electromagnetic oscillations in the 4–10 Hz range.

The major area concerning states of consciousness on which the electro-magnetic theory as it stands does not provide much explanatory power is the difference between waking and dreaming. These states can not be readily distinguished by gross examination of brain-generated electro-magnetic patterns at this point. However, since both waking and dreaming do involve conscious experiences, this defect may be seen as one of detail rather than of major substance. From one point of view, the distinction between waking and dreaming has more to do with the specific contents of the conscious experiences than anything—and our theory has so far been at least partly successful in showing why the conscious contents of the dream state differ from those of the waking state (in terms of the prevention by the thalamus of sensory input from reaching the cortex).

CHAPTER THREE: SMELL

❖ *Do there exist spatiotemporal configurations of the electromagnetic field that covary with olfactory consciousness?*

This chapter asks the question "does the brain generate patterns in the electromagnetic field that correlate with olfactory sensations?" The answer is an unequivocal "yes."

Olfaction, the sense of smell, is probably the most ancient of all the sensory systems. The first cells, arising at the dawn of life billions of years ago, very likely had a rudimentary capacity for sampling the chemical qualities of the environment. Certainly modern bacteria such as *Escherichia coli* possess finely tuned receptors for various environmental chemicals. They also have the means for transducing the stimuli, decoding, integrating and transmitting information about them and for generating appropriate behavioral responses. The earliest chemoreception systems in multicellular organisms can be found in coelenterates. With further evolution, chemoreception became the function of specialized cells grouped in specific areas of the epithelium. As early in the phylogenetic tree as molluscs and crustaceans, these groups of receptor cells project to structures called olfactory glomeruli, which are clustered in olfactory bulbs not unlike those found in more advanced vertebrates. In fact it has been persuasively argued that olfactory systems quite similar to those of contemporary insects and vertebrates were probably already in place 500 million years ago, conveying exquisite sensitivity to the identities of places, trails, individuals, prey, predators, mates, social groups and food (Hildebrand, 1995). Thus, if we are interested in the evolution of conscious perceptions, the olfactory system must be an excellent place to start.

Electromagnetic patterns in olfaction

Lord Adrian (Adrian, 1950) was the first to postulate that classes of odors should be correlated with spatial patterns of neural activity in the olfactory receptor layer and olfactory bulb. The inference from Adrian's original hypothesis was that for each kind of odor, there should exist a unique spatial pattern of neural activity in the olfactory bulb. This pattern should be present when and only when a particular odor is present. In fact Adrian's prediction has been born out startlingly well for invertebrates and in line with our current hypothesis the firing patterns that correlate with particular odors turn out to be not merely spatial patterns, but spatiotemporal patterns. In mammals, however, the situation is somewhat more complex (which is perhaps predictable, considering that mammals have more complex minds than insects). The correlation in rabbits, for example, is not between spatiotemporal electromagnetic patterns and the properties of the stimulus, but between spatiotemporal electromagnetic patterns and the meaning the stimulus has for the animal.

The overall anatomical design of the early processing stages of the olfactory system is remarkably similar in insects and in humans—only the names of the various structures are different. In both systems the point of contact with the environment is the olfactory receptor cells (ORCs). These are located in the epithelium of the antennae in insects, or the nose in humans, where each nostril contains 10^7 to 10^8 of them (Freeman, 1972). Generally speaking, each ORC reacts to a specific kind of odorant (although this specificity is far from absolute) and only a few molecules of odorant may be necessary to elicit a reaction. The ORCs reacting to any one odorant are spread more or less evenly throughout the area of olfactory epithelium (with some general grouping so that broad classes of odorant are more represented in some areas of epithelium than in others), so the overall outcome is that different odorants stimulate different patterns of ORCs in the antenna or nose. Thus, although smell is not a spatial sense in the same way that sight is, the initial representation of an odor stimulus in the olfactory pathway does have a spatial structure.

In the second stage of the olfactory system, olfactory receptor cells project to regions of the brain called the antennal lobe in insects or the olfactory bulb in mammals. Here projections from the different odor-specific ORCs are collected into odor-specific groupings, in structures called olfactory glomeruli. In humans, each glomerulus receives about 10^4 receptor axons (Freeman, 1991a). Thus there is a second, differently organized spatial mapping of odor information in the antennal lobe or the olfactory bulb. This mapping is odotopic, rather than somatotopic.

Finally, there are projections from the insect antennal lobe or the mammalian olfactory bulb to the mushroom body in insects or to a series of primary cortical areas in mammals. Here the mapping takes on a temporal as well as a spatial aspect.

Insect Olfaction

In locusts, three interacting phenomena have been observed in connection with the representation of odors in the mushroom body (Laurent, 1996):

(1)   When an odorant is puffed onto the locust's antennae, extracellular recordings from the mushroom body show oscillatory local field potentials that have a frequency of 20–30 Hz. These oscillations occur without a phase gradient over the whole mushroom body calyx and last for the duration of the odor puff or slightly longer. Within any one locust, the oscillations are at least macroscopically the same for all odors. Hence on a large scale they can not be regarded as carrying any information about the nature of the odor, only the fact that an odor is present.

(2)   Within these mass oscillations can be distinguished the second phenomenon. Odors are repeatably and reliably represented by the firing of particular ensembles of the neurons that project from the antennal lobe to the mushroom body. In other words, a

particular odor elicits the firing of a particular group of projection neurons. Any given projection neuron can participate in several different odor-specific ensembles, but a certain group of projection neurons always fires in response to presentation of any given odor. This means that there is a spatial pattern of neuronal firing associated with each odor. However, as well as this spatial pattern, there is also a temporal pattern of neuronal firing associated with each odor. This is generated by the fact that not all the projection neurons which fire in response to a particular odor do so at the same time. Some fire mostly at the beginning of the odor presentation, some at the end, some only in the middle, some at the beginning and the end but not in the middle, and so on. These temporal firing patterns are consistent in each neuron for each odor (at the same concentration of odorant). In other words, any particular projection neuron always behaves the same way in response to one particular odor.

The overall outcome is that any given odorant elicits a very specific spatiotemporal pattern of firing of the neurons projecting to the mushroom body (Laurent, Wehr, & Davidowitz, 1996). The temporal aspect of the pattern dictates that the spatial aspect of the pattern evolves over the course of the stimulus presentation.

(3) Additionally, there is a third layer of complexity to the stimulus representation. It is likely that a neuron in the mushroom body will fire in response to synaptic input from a projection neuron only if this synaptic input occurs at a time when the mushroom body cell is at a stage in the mass field potential oscillation when it is relatively depolarised. Since not all of the action potentials in the projection neurons are phase-locked to the macroscopic 20 Hz oscillations in the mushroom body, not all of the action potentials in the projection neurons will induce firing of mushroom body neurons. The situation becomes somewhat circular

here, because there is some evidence suggesting that the mushroom body oscillations themselves are likely caused, at least in part, by fluctuating synaptic input from the projection neurons. Cause and effect are difficult to distinguish in this complex situation, but the upshot is that because the effective input from projection neurons to the mushroom body evolves over the course of the stimulus presentation, *there is a smaller-scale spatiotemporal structure within the envelope of the macroscopic 20-ish Hz oscillation which does carry repeatable and reliable information about the characteristics of the odor.*

This looks suspiciously as though what we are dealing with is a 20-Hz carrier wave, which could plausibly be identified with olfactory consciousness *per se*, plus a series of amplitude and frequency modulations of the carrier wave which covary with the contents of olfactory consciousness.

Some slightly disturbing implications

But wait a moment. All this refers only to the humble locust. At the best of times, one can never be certain even that other humans experience things in the same way as one does oneself (and indeed the vicissitudes and misunderstandings of everyday life tend to suggest that they often do not). So, taking into account the fact that locusts are very small and don't actually look much like humans, it may be regarded as a moot point whether such insects can be allowed to claim even the most rudimentary form of our own highly evolved Consciousness. The relevance of the above results to our quest might reasonably be questioned.

However, as we will soon see, remarkably similar experimental results have been obtained from rabbits, rats and cats. Such creatures are relatively large, pleasantly furry and much more often the subject of anthropomorphic children's stories than are insects (*pace* Jiminy Cricket). In short, they are animals to which one is altogether more inclined to accord the benefit of the doubt, consciousness-wise.

This is mildly disturbing. If the olfactory system of locusts works in the same way as that of cats, and if we are willing to allow that cats possess, if not intellectual brilliance, at least simple consciousness, then we are forced to contemplate the idea that locusts may also have a similar consciousness to our own, at least when it comes to the basic raw feel of smell sensations. Of course because insects are so much smaller, there would be less of it in an absolute sense, this putative consciousness. So maybe we can still regard it as OK to squash mosquitos, because in squashing a mosquito one is only squashing a very tiny aliquot of a very simple sort of consciousness. Well, maybe it's OK to squash mosquitos (or to eat rabbits or cows) anyway, because that's just the natural way of the animal kingdom—everything kills and/or eats anything else that is not a member of its own species, if it can. That mosquito was eating us, after all…Before such outrageously unscientific ruminations go any further however, we should also admit the idea that this kind of spatiotemporal coding may be merely the pre-conscious activity of the nervous system. Perhaps there is more to consciousness than low frequency spatiotemporally modulated electromagnetic oscillations.

Let us examine the evidence from rabbits, rats and cats.

Mammalian Olfaction

Because mammals have hugely more neurons than insects, it is no longer feasible to measure large-scale patterns of neural firing in mammals by single-cell recording techniques. Extracellular measurements of so-called "field potentials" must be used. Field potentials are just spatial summations of the electromagnetic field changes caused by the more-or-less simultaneous firing of large groups or masses of neurons.

When field potentials are recorded from an array of chronically implanted electrodes in the olfactory bulb of rabbits, cats, or rats, macroscopic oscillations similar to those described in the locust are measured. The frequency of the oscillations is within the gamma range, but the details vary with the species—in rats the oscillations are at about

52 Hz, in rabbits about 56 Hz and in cats around 38 Hz (Bressler &
Freeman, 1980). Thus, given that the comparable oscillations in locusts
are at about 20 Hz, there does not appear to be any consistent correlation
between oscillation frequency and size of animal.

Notably, these oscillations in mammalian olfactory bulbs have a global
character. This is shown by a high level of wave form similarity across the
extent of the rabbit olfactory bulb and also within a large portion of the
prepyriform cortex, to which the olfactory bulb projects (Bressler, 1984).
Such a global quality sits well with requirement 4 in Chapter 1, where it is
argued that consciousness *per se* has a global character and thus that the
neural correlate of consciousness should have a global character. Further, if
we assume for the moment that these global oscillations are identical with
olfactory consciousness, the different frequencies of the oscillation in different species of animal would suggest that in general, what it is like to
smell is different for cats than it is for rabbits, and that it is different again
for rats. On the other hand, what it is like for one rabbit to smell is probably quite similar to what it is like for another rabbit to smell (with certain
provisos which will be seen in the next paragraphs). These ideas are,
perhaps, not counterintuitive.

At this stage however, the similarity between insects and mammals
starts to break down. Early experiments involving simple presentation of
odors to rabbits (Freeman, 1978) failed to elicit any invariant odor-
specific modulations of the global carrier oscillations. With the benefit of
hindsight, it appears likely that the real reason for this is that suitable
methods of signal processing and pattern recognition had not yet been
developed, but at the time the other theoretical possibility, which was that
the rabbits may not actually have been consciously experiencing odor-
specific sensations, (either because they were not paying attention or
because they were physiologically incapable of smelling certain odors) also
seemed compelling. Because of this possibility, a training procedure that
would allow unequivocal inference from behavior that the animals had
perceived and discriminated particular odors was adopted. Thus the more

mathematically sophisticated later experiments in this series measure not only sensation *per se*, but also memory and recognition processes and presumably motor processes preparatory for the trained movements. This may be seen as unfortunate for our search for electromagnetic correlates of sensation *per se*, or it may be fortunate in that it simply reflects the real situation, which may be that odors are not actually experienced in any stable and repeatable way until they can be recognized or identified. At any rate, what we now have are some excellent data from experiments in which animals were trained to associate certain odors with the expectation of reward or punishment, and so to behave accordingly when they identified those smells.

The results of a series of experiments designed to identify odor-specific patterns in the EEG recorded from an array of 64 electrodes implanted over the olfactory bulb of rabbits that had been trained to discriminate particular odors are reported in three classic papers (Freeman & Baird, 1987; Freeman & Grajski, 1987; Freeman & Viana Di Prisco, 1986). A number of mathematically sophisticated pattern recognition techniques were applied to the raw data obtained in these experiments in order to identify odor-specific patterns, and since the results are so important to the overall argument put forward in this book, it is probably valuable to have at least some non-mathematical understanding of these techniques.

The basic problem facing the experimenters was that there was no clear prior idea of what the odor-specific patterns might look like, or where or when they might exist in the olfactory bulb. Therefore the rationale guiding the development of the EEG processing and pattern recognition procedures was essentially an *ad hoc* one. First, it was assumed that patterns existed in the EEG which were distinctly different for (a) odors the animals had been conditioned to react to (b) odors they had been conditioned not to react to, and (c) a control condition of no presented odor. Then any mathematical algorithm that helped in correctly classifying EEG segments as having been recorded during one or other of these stimulus conditions was adopted.

The first step in the analysis was to apply some general signal processing techniques, designed to smooth the data and remove trends that had no connection with the patterns being searched for. This involved replacing data from bad channels (those that produced obvious artifacts) with the average of 2 adjacent channels, temporal smoothing of the data from each channel (taking the mean of each time point plus its 2 adjacent time points weighted by 0.5) and "detrending" of the data to remove the underlying respiratory wave. Then began the serious data reduction.

First, the average time series for all 64 electrodes (the time ensemble average) was calculated. This completely removed spatial information. A Fast Fourier Transform (FFT) of this time ensemble average[1] gave information that allowed fitting of an amplitude and frequency modulated cosine wave to the time ensemble average. The data that were not fitted (the residuals) were fitted by another cosine wave, and so on for the first five fits. Thus the ensemble average time series was decomposed into five components. The one that carried most of the power (usually the first) was called the dominant component. This manipulation identified two kinds of burst occurring when odors were presented. The first had a dominant frequency greater than 55 Hz and one narrow dominant spectral peak (i.e. not much frequency modulation). The second type of burst had a dominant frequency less than 55 Hz and was disorderly, with broad spectral patterns. A behavioral assay showed that the high- and not the low-frequency bursts carried odor-specific information.

Now the same sort of averaging procedure was performed in the spatial domain. For each of the 64 electrodes, the root mean square of the amplitude of the whole sample of EEG collected for each odor condition was calculated. This gave 64 numbers, each of which represented the average voltage for the whole recording time at one of the 64 points in space

---

1   FFTs break a signal down into a series of simple sine waves of different frequencies and show how much the sine wave at each frequency contributes to the original complex signal.

where the electrodes were recording. At this very crude level of spatial analysis, it was found (not surprisingly) that there was no correlation between the odor condition and the spatial pattern. Instead, it turned out that each rabbit had a characteristic spatial pattern that was like an individual signature; never exactly the same twice, but still easily recognizable (Freeman & Grajski, 1987).

In order to pull odor-specific information out of the spatial patterns, it was found necessary to go back to the original data and perform several further processing steps, involving both temporal and spatial filtering and also a mathematical procedure called spatial deconvolution. First, the two different types of burst (those with a dominant frequency greater than 55 Hz and those with a dominant frequency less than 55 Hz) were processed separately. This was a vital step, because as it turned out, the orderly >55Hz bursts carried odor-specific spatial information while the disorderly <55Hz bursts did not. Secondly, it was hypothesized that synaptic currents in the granule cells (the inhibitory cells in the olfactory bulb) constituted the signal in this context while far-field currents from other neurons were noise. Therefore, spatial filters were developed to identify and enhance the contribution of the granule cells. This turned out to be equivalent to applying a low-pass spatial filter. This manipulation showed that while *high frequencies in the time series carried the information, low frequencies (0.15 to 0.25 cycles/mm) in the spatial series carried the information.*

Thirdly, a mathematical procedure called spatial deconvolution was used. This was designed to correct the distortion caused by volume conduction (i.e. partially to undo the blurring that inevitably occurred because measurements could only be taken at the surface of the olfactory bulb and not deep in the bulb where the electromagnetic patterns were generated). Finally, the data were normalized to remove the effect of each rabbit's individual "signature".

Out of all this processing, some very interesting facts emerged.

(1) Odor-specific spatial patterns were detectable in the olfactory bulb of rabbits trained to discriminate between two odors.

(2) Most interestingly, the odor-specific information was not localizable to subsets of channels. On the one hand, deletion of channels decreased the power of the remaining channel data to classify bursts correctly. But on the other hand, subsets of as few as 16 randomly selected channels had the power to classify bursts correctly at better than chance levels. This suggests that the information was broadly distributed over the bulb. Other results suggested that the granule cell activity patterns that contained odor-specific information extended well beyond the limits of the array window of observation. In particular, the phase gradient suggested that they involved the entire main bulb.

Thus *the discriminative output of the bulb apparently involved the entire structure, even though the receptor input was delivered to limited subsets of mitral cells in the bulb.*

(3) Overall burst amplitude played a role in separating odor from control bursts, but no role in separating bursts occurring during presentation of different odors.

(4) The frequency and phase properties played no role.

(5) The amplitude properties that determine the characteristic signature of each animal played no role.

(6) In the words of the authors (Freeman & Baird, 1987) "During learning to identify an odor, it appears that a nerve cell assembly is formed by strengthened connections among the mitral cells that are coactivated by the odor under reinforcement... Thereafter, the arrival of the odor may lead to formation of a stereotypic spatial pattern over the entire bulb as a necessary albeit insufficient condition for correct response to that odor. On this interpretation, the bulbar output is not localized but is truly

global; every neuron participates in every learned odor response but in differing degrees for different odors."

These experiments, then, seem to suggest that there do exist electromagnetic field patterns which can be used to classify correctly the olfactory sensations being experienced by the animals from which the patterns were recorded. But how do these results stack up against the ground rules laid out in Chapter 1?

In the methodological arena, the experiments pass with flying colors the requirements concerning elimination of artefacts and control of general physiological factors. They fare less well when it comes to the necessity to isolate consciousness *per se* from other brain processes—in particular, they deliberately conflate conscious experience with memory. However, all of the general requirements specified under the rules of evidence for identifying an electromagnetic pattern with a specific subjective experience are indeed fulfilled:

1. In as far as this can possibly be ascertained using non-verbal subjects, the spatial electromagnetic patterns were certainly present when and only when the subject was conscious of a particular experience. This was shown by the fact that the patterns were only present when the rabbit responded behaviorally to the presence of a particular odorant. There was no odorant-specific spatial pattern in the absence of an odorant, and in cases when the odorant was present but there was no behavioral response (presumably because the rabbit was not paying attention) the dominant burst frequency was less than 55 Hz and there was no odorant-specific spatial pattern of amplitudes.

2. The electromagnetic patterns certainly did correlate with subjective experience rather than with the physical stimulus. In fact, as the experimenters put it, "the spatial patterns lacked invariance with respect to odorant conditioned stimuli, showing instead a dependence on brain state, behavioral context and training history" (Barrie,

Freeman, & Lenhart, 1996; Freeman, 1991a). In other words, the patterns correlated with the meaning the stimulus had for the animal, not with the stimulus itself. Furthermore, although it was not directly demonstrated that the spatial amplitude pattern in the bulb varied according to sensation rather than odorant concentration, dynamic range compression compatible with Weber's Law (see Appendix A) was shown to occur at the input stage to the olfactory bulb (Freeman, 1991a).

(3)   The electromagnetic patterns were certainly generated by a relatively localized area of the brain.

(4)   But they had a striking global quality. This was shown by the facts that (a) almost as much information was carried by the pattern recorded using an array of only 16 electrodes as was carried by the full array of 64 electrodes and (b) there were no "edge effects" i.e. channels at the edge of the array were just as useful information-wise as those in the middle. One likely interpretation of these observations is that the overall electromagnetic pattern in the whole olfactory bulb was the important thing, not any smaller-scale, localized part of this. The explanation of the lack of edge effects would then be that the overall size of the important pattern was significantly larger than the electrode array, so that edge effects would not be expected in this sub-sample of the main pattern. We can also say that the spatial resolution of the pattern must have been such that in an array of the size used, the number of sampling points could be reduced to as few as 16 before spatial aliasing became a problem.

Summary

In the mammalian olfactory system, the existence of spatiotemporal electromagnetic patterns that obey almost all of the criteria in Chapter 1 has been unequivocally demonstrated.

CHAPTER FOUR: HEARING

❧ *Do there exist spatiotemporal configurations of the electromagnetic field that covary with auditory consciousness?*

This chapter asks the question "does the brain generate patterns in the electromagnetic field that correlate with auditory sensations?" The answer is again "yes."

Spatial electromagnetic patterns and auditory experience

Again work from Walter Freeman's lab leads the way in answering the question addressed in this chapter (Barrie, Freeman, & Lenhart, 1996). The experiments in this case were structured as follows.

In each of 5 rabbits, an array of 64 electrodes spaced 0.79 mm apart was implanted over the left auditory cortex, under surgical anesthesia. After a week's convalescence, each rabbit was then classically conditioned to discriminate between two kinds of 100 ms tones, one of 500 Hz and the other 5,000 Hz. The conditioning paradigm used a brief electric shock delivered to the cheek 3 seconds after one or the other of the two kinds of tone. The tone that was paired with the shock was called the conditioned stimulus (CS+) and the tone that was not paired with the shock was called the unconditioned stimulus (CS-). Rabbits learned to associate the CS+ with the shock within three or four trials, as evidenced by a change in their breathing as soon as they heard the tone that was going to be followed by a shock. Three weeks after the start of the experiment, the shock was switched to association with the other kind of tone. As before, the rationale for this conditioning procedure was that it provided unequivocal behavioral evidence that the rabbits were hearing and discriminating particular stimuli.

When a rabbit had learned a particular discrimination, each tone was played into its headphones 20 times, randomly sequenced in inter-trial interval and stimulus order, to yield a 40–record experiment. Each time a tone was delivered, three seconds worth of EEG was recorded before and three seconds after the stimulus. Then an impressive panoply of pattern recognition procedures were applied to the data, off-line.

The results were similar to those found in the olfactory system, with two major differences. First, no breathing-related EEG activity was found in the auditory system, as it was in the olfactory system. Secondly, a temporal EEG pattern time-locked to the stimulus was detectable in the auditory system. This was not the case in the olfactory system, where responses were time-locked to inhalations rather than to stimulus onset.

The results with regard to pattern classification did mimic those seen in the olfactory system. After normalization and suitable spatial and tempo-ral filtering, the spatial patterns of EEG amplitude recorded across the array of electrodes could be classified at greater than 99% accuracy as being associated with either the negatively reinforced tone (CS+) or the unreinforced tone (CS-). As with the olfactory results, these spatial patterns did not correlate strictly with the kind of stimulus, but with the meaning the stimulus had for the animal. For example, the spatial pattern evoked by a 500 Hz tone was constant between week 1 and week 2 of the experiment, but changed in week 3 when this tone changed from being the CS- to being the CS+ (or vice versa). Unfortunately the question of whether the spatial pattern evoked by a 500 Hz CS+ tone was different from the spatial pattern evoked by a 5,000 Hz CS+ tone is not explicitly answered in this paper, although the data were presumably available to conduct that analysis. The answer would be very interesting, because it would show whether the patterns simply reflected an emotional response to a conditioned stimulus, or whether they correlated with a particular stimulus plus the emotional response to it.

Again as in olfactory system, the pattern information in these auditory experiments was not localized to any particular set of recording electrodes.

The whole array consisted of 64 electrodes, but as few as 16 randomly selected channels were all that were necessary to correlate the electromagnetic patterns with the conditions under which they were recorded. Also, no "edges" were detected for the spatial patterns, in the sense of channels near the margins of the arrays having less information for the classification of the patterns than those in the center. The authors of the study interpret these findings as evidence that the patterns resembled the distributed representation in a hologram, in that the same information seemed to be present on every channel, with the resolution depending on the number of channels available but not on their location. In my opinion a more likely scenario is simply the interpretation given at the end of Chapter 3: that the pattern as a whole is the important thing, and the area occupied by the fluctuations defining the pattern was large enough so that the density of channels could be reduced from a total of 64 in the given area to as few as 16 before spatial aliasing occurred. The physical size of the electrode arrays in these experiments was of the order of 6 mm x 6 mm, so the lack of edge effect suggests that overall size of the relevant pattern was probably larger than 36 mm^2. This insight that the pattern as a whole is the factor defining a conscious experience fits with the postulated need for patterns correlating with consciousness to have a global quality.

Methodologically, these experiments stack up against the suggested requirements in Chapter 1 in much the same way as do the olfactory experiments described in Chapter 3. The experiments are well controlled in terms of artefact rejection, and in terms of keeping general physiological variables (with the important exception of arousal) constant. However they do deliberately conflate both memory processes and the emotional effects of the conditioned stimulus (i.e. expectation of an electric shock) with the subjects' simple conscious experience of auditory sensations. The experimenters adopted the procedures that resulted in this latter feature for good reasons: (a) it was necessary to ask the subjects whether or not they had experienced a certain sensation, and since rabbits can't talk they had to be asked this question by a more circuitous method, and (b) human subjects can talk, but it would have been much more difficult both ethically and practically to implant an array of electrodes on the pial surface of a human subject. The reason it was better to implant electrodes on the pial surface than on the scalp was that electromagnetic patterns are significantly blurred by the time they reach the scalp because of volume conduction through the skull, and this blurring could be expected to impede spatial pattern recognition. However, whatever the excellence of the reasons, the outcome was that significantly more than simple sensations were measured in these experiments.

Let us, then, examine some instances of spatiotemporal electromagnetic patterns which correlate with auditory sensations in human subjects, who can be asked directly about their experience. As mentioned, spatial electric field patterns are seriously blurred when recorded non-invasively at the scalp and in any case the time after a discrete stimulus at which the corresponding sensation is experienced is likely to be quite important. So to start with, we will switch our attention from the spatial patterns that are correlated with particular experiences to temporal patterns.

Temporal electromagnetic patterns and auditory experience

In all sensory modalities, it is possible to record by electroencephalography (EEG) or magnetoencephalography (MEG) a stereotyped series of waves that are time-locked to a sensory stimulus. These are called evoked potentials, because they are evoked by a stimulus. When the stimulus is auditory, they are called auditory evoked potentials (AEPs).

Since the amplitude of evoked potentials is very small compared with the amplitude of the total EEG or MEG, it is usually necessary to average the responses to a number of successive stimuli in order to pull the waves that are evoked by the stimulus out of the general EEG "noise". This stimulus-locked averaging procedure is a commonly used trick for extracting signal from noise, which basically works because at any given time point after a stimulus, random noise is equally likely to be positive or negative and so over a few hundred trials it averages out to be zero. The signal, on the other hand, is always the same (always positive or always negative) at any given time post-stimulus and therefore it is not affected by averaging. Thus the averaging procedure suppresses noise (or at least all those signals that are random with respect to the stimulus) and allows identification of the EEG waves which are evoked by the stimulus.

Averaging produces a series of peaks and troughs which are more or less constant over all normally hearing human adults (with the proviso that in the middle latency section of the response, the negative/positive Na/Pa complex is consistently observed in normal subjects but all the other waves are variable in latency and morphology, as well as frequency of occurrence across subjects (Mendel & Goldstein, 1971; Ozdamar & Kraus, 1983; Picton, Hillyard, Krausz, & Galambos, 1974; Streletz, Katz, Hohenberger, & Cracco, 1977)). These peaks and troughs of the evoked potential are given names, not because they are necessarily generated by particular discrete neural events (for example the N1 a.k.a. N100 wave is thought to have at least six different neural generators (Naatanen & Picton, 1987)) but because they are convenient points for measurement. Notwithstanding this however, it is possible to make hypotheses about the functions of whatever neural activity generates the various waves.

Data given in the following sections support the proposal that the parts of the AEP that correlate with the simple conscious experience of an auditory stimulus are the waves of the middle latency response, particularly those occurring 30 to 50 ms after the stimulus. Waves earlier than this are proposed to be the correlates of preconscious processing and later waves are proposed to correlate with various processes underlying perceptual functions such as working memory, comparisons with previous stimuli and orienting to novel events. While all of these latter functions may be regarded as vital to the generation of consciousness in the broader sense, it is argued that simple "raw" conscious sensation corresponds to the neural activity underlying the middle latency waves of the evoked potential.

The following sections providing evidence for this contention will be numbered in the same way as the requirements set out in Chapter 1 for identifying an electromagnetic pattern with a specific subjective experience.

Evidence that middle latency waves of the auditory evoked potential correlate with simple sensation

1.1 (i) (a) Auditory evoked potentials and removal of the physical stimulus

By definition, auditory evoked potentials do not occur when there is no physical auditory stimulus with which to time-lock the averaging process. In a test of inter- and intra-judge reliability of visual scoring of the auditory middle latency response, it became increasingly difficult to detect middle latency responses as the intensity of the stimulus decreased, but silent controls were always identified as response absent (Mendel, Saraca, & Gerber, 1984). Thus this requirement is certainly fulfilled.

1.1 (i) (b) Auditory evoked potentials and blocking of the ears

To my knowledge there is no published evidence specifically saying that the requirement is fulfilled. It seems very likely that it would be.

1.1 (i) (c) Auditory evoked potentials and sensation threshold

Both the auditory brainstem response (ABR) and the middle latency response (MLR) have been used clinically for predicting subjective auditory threshold. In other words, when the intensity of the physical stimulus is turned right down, both these waveforms have very similar thresholds to the subjective threshold for hearing an auditory sensation. Of the two waveforms, middle latency responses are the better predictors of sensation threshold (Picton & Durieux-Smith, 1988). Prediction of pure tone subjective thresholds from tone-pip MLR thresholds is more accurate than that from click ABR thresholds (Xu, Vel, Vinck, & Cauwenberge, 1996). MLR thresholds are thus reported as being useful for objectively assessing the hearing of compensation claimants for occupational noise-induced hearing loss.

The steady state form of the middle latency response (i.e. the response elicited by presentation of stimuli at 40 Hz) has also been shown in a number of studies to have a threshold similar to the sensation threshold (Galambos, Makeig, & Talmachoff, 1981; Stapells, Linden, Suffield, Hamel, & Picton, 1984; Stapells, Makeig, & Galambos, 1987).

Later waves of the AEP such as N1 and P2 do not correlate with sensation threshold. Breathing concentrations of nitrous oxide sufficient to increase the threshold for eliciting N1 and P2 and to decrease their amplitude by an amount equivalent to a 30 dB reduction in stimulus intensity was observed to have no effect whatsoever on subjective auditory pure-tone threshold (Houston, McClelland, & Fenwick, 1988). Thus the subjective act of hearing appears to be unrelated to the amplitude or latency of either N1 or P2.

1.1 (i) (d) Auditory evoked potentials and habituation to repetitive stimuli

When the frequency of discrete auditory stimuli such as clicks is turned up, some waves of the auditory evoked potential "habituate" or disappear after a certain repetition frequency is reached, even though the subject still reports accurately hearing the discrete sounds. These waves clearly do not represent conscious sensations *per se*.

Waves N1 (around 100 ms) and P1 or Pb (around 50–80 ms) fall into this category. The amplitude of P1 has been reported to decline when the stimulus rate exceeds 1 Hz, while subjective detectability of clicks presented at more than 1 per second clearly does not (Erwin & Buchwald, 1986). In this study the filter used was 10–300 Hz, a bandpass which has been shown to introduce artifacts in a similar study (Jones & Baxter, 1988). However a second study (Freedman, Adler, Waldo, Pachtman, & Franks, 1983), which used a much wider pass band (1–1000 Hz), also found that the amplitude of P1 decreased by 80% in response to a second stimulus 0.5 ms after the first (in normal subjects, but not in schizophrenics). It thus seems likely that P1 correlates with some sort of non-conscious processing rather than with raw auditory sensation.

Wave N1 likewise declines or disappears completely at stimulus rates which are clearly detectable subjectively. Many studies, reviewed by Naatanen and Picton (Naatanen & Picton, 1987), show that auditory N1 waves are exceptionally sensitive to the rate at which stimuli are presented. N1 habituates quickly in response to stimuli more frequent than about 0.1 Hz, and at this frequency stimuli are quite clearly audible as separate events.

Stimulus rate does not significantly affect the amplitude of Pa, however (Tucker & Ruth, 1996). There is no change in Pa amplitude at least up to a stimulus repetition rate of 11 Hz. This is consistent with the hypothesis that Pa is correlated with subjective sound sensation, while N1 is not.

1.1 (i) (e) Auditory evoked potentials and anesthesia

It has been suggested (Pockett, 1999) that the response of the various waves of the auditory evoked potential to the induction of and recovery from general anesthesia shows that simple auditory sensation corresponds to the middle latency waves of the AEP. The argument for this is a multi-partite one, which runs as follows.

There are two main classes of general anesthetics; the non-specific and the receptor specific anesthetics. Commonly used non-specific agents include the anesthetic gases halothane, enflurane and isoflurane, and the injectible agent propofol. These agents probably act in a non-specific way by changing the fluidity of neuronal cell membranes. Commonly used receptor-specific agents include the analgesic *opioids* (e.g. fentanyl, sufentanil and alfentanil), the anxiolytic *benzodiazepines* (e.g. diazepam a.k.a. Valium, flunitrazepam and midazolam), the sleep-inducing *barbiturates* (e.g. sodium pentothal, methohexital and pentobarbital) and the dissociative anesthetic *ketamine*. Each of these classes of receptor-specific agents is known to act on a particular class of neurotransmitter receptors in the brain. In general, non-specific and receptor-specific anesthetic agents induce different states of consciousness and have concomitantly different effects on auditory evoked potentials.

The waves of the auditory evoked potential that occur earlier than 10 ms post-stimulus are called the auditory brainstem response (ABR), because they originate in the brainstem. The ABR is at least grossly unaffected by clinical anesthesia due to a wide variety of general anesthetics (Hall, 1990), so it is unlikely to represent the neural correlates of auditory consciousness.

The waves of the middle latency response (MLR), however, are significantly affected when consciousness is lost during general anesthesia of the sort that is induced by non-specific anesthetics. Halothane, enflurane, isoflurane and propofol all cause a progressive reduction of the waves Na, Pa and Nb as concentration of the anesthetic increases. This decrease in Na, Pa and Nb is well correlated with a reduction in awareness, as measured by response to a verbal command to raise a finger or squeeze the experimenter's hand (Davies, Mantzaridis, Kenny, & Fisher, 1996; Newton, et al., 1992; Thornton, Heneghan, James, & Jones, 1984).

In contrast, receptor specific anesthetics from the benzodiazepine and opioid classes do not necessarily affect the auditory middle latency response, even in doses which do abolish both responsiveness to verbal command and the formation of explicit memories (Schwender, Faber-Zullig, Klasing, Poppel, & Peter, 1994; Schwender, Kaiser, Klasing, Peter, & Poppel, 1994; Schwender, Klasing, Madler, Poppel, & Peter, 1993a; Schwender, et al., 1993). Unlike the non-specific anesthetics studied however, the receptor specific anesthetics in these experiments did preserve significant motor signs of wakefulness, such as coughing, blinking and purposeful movements of the limbs. Also, it was clearly shown in these experiments that the formation of implicit memories for auditory material was correlated with preservation of auditory mid-latency responses. There is a case to be made that the only things that are abolished by the combination of opioids and benzodiazepines that is usually administered when light anesthesia is desirable clinically are pain, explicit memory formation and any sense of things mattering, such as would cause one to bother responding to a command to squeeze someone's hand (which is the general test used to assess awareness). This accords with the generally expressed opinion of working anesthetists that the state induced by opioid/benzodiazepine treatment is not "anesthesia" *per se*, although it does allow surgical interventions to be performed without causing the patient distress. Thus it is highly likely that light opioid/benzodiazepine "anesthesia" allows a level of awareness of auditory sensations which is not present in the deeper anesthesia induced by non-specific anesthetics.

A third anesthetic state, different from either of the two described above, is induced by the so-called "dissociative" receptor-specific anesthetic ketamine. Ketamine is known to cause unpleasant dreams or hallucinations of a sort that are not reported with the other varieties of anesthetic (White, Way, & Trevor, 1982) and there is some justification for regarding the ketamine-induced state as more akin to a dream-ridden sleep from which one cannot awaken, than to anesthesia. As might be predicted if this were the case (see the section on auditory evoked potentials and sleep) ketamine has little obvious effect on the transient form of the auditory middle latency response (Schwender, et al., 1994; Schwender, Klasing, Madler, Poppel, & Peter, 1993b) and is reported to actually increase the amplitude of the auditory steady state response evoked by presentation of auditory stimuli at 40Hz (Plourde, Baribeau, & Bonhomme, 1997). It may well be that externally driven auditory experience still occurs during ketamine intoxication (as it does during REM sleep), but that the auditory sensations are not processed in quite the same way as they are in the normal waking state, being instead incorporated into ongoing dreams.

So all of the above evidence fits the proposal that simple sensory awareness covaries with the amplitude of middle latency auditory evoked potentials. Less work has been done on the effects of anesthetics on the later waves in the auditory evoked potential. In general, later components of the AEP are more sensitive to anesthetics than the middle latency components (deBeer, et al., 1996), but it appears that their disappearance on induction of anesthesia and reappearance on recovery does not correlate at all well with the disappearance and reappearance of auditory sensation.

One study (Houston, McClelland, & Fenwick, 1988) found that concentrations of nitrous oxide which did affect the threshold for the production of N1 and P2 waves of the auditory evoked potential did not affect the subjective threshold for detection of a soft sound. Another study (Plourde & Picton, 1991) found that when patients were asked to press a button on hearing a particular sound during induction of anesthesia, correctly detected sounds (hits) did evoke N1 and P3 waves, whereas undetected sounds (misses) did not. This suggests that N1 and P3 do correlate with auditory sensation. However during emergence from anesthesia in this study (a) there was generally a small N1 and occasionally also a small P3 for misses and (b) neither N1 nor P3 were necessarily present when a correct hit was scored. Thus these later waves of the auditory evoked potential were sometimes present when there was no awareness of the sound and sometimes absent when there was awareness of the sound. This evidence suggests that N1 and P3 waves represent some feature of auditory processing other than raw sensory awareness of the sound.

1.1 (i) (f) Auditory evoked potentials and sleep

The story of what various different investigators have reported as happening to middle latency auditory evoked potentials during sleep boils down to a cautionary tale about the artefacts that can be introduced by over-zealous band-pass filtering of the EEG. Early studies (e.g. that of Erwin and Buchwald, 1986) used filters with a rather restricted pass band (10–300 Hz) and reported no change in the middle latency waves Pa (30–40 ms) or Nb (45–55 ms) during any stage of sleep. Only the Pb component occurring between 55 and 80 ms was reported to disappear during slow wave sleep. However a slightly later study (Jones & Baxter, 1988) using a less restrictive pass band (0.3–3000 Hz) reported significant increases in the latency of Pa and sometimes complete disappearance of Nb during stages 2 and 3/4 of sleep. This latter study shows a sobering comparison between data recorded with a wide-bandpass filter and the same data after it has been digitally filtered using the more restrictive band-pass used in the earlier study and demonstrates how an artifact introduced by the tighter filter gives the erroneous impression that little change occurs in the amplitudes of Pa and Nb during slow wave sleep. A second study using a wide filter (Deiber, Ibanez, Bastuji, Fischer, & Mauguiere, 1989) again shows changes in Pa, Nb and Pb components of the auditory evoked potential in sleep. During stage 2 sleep, both latency and amplitude of Pa increased and neither Nb nor Pb could be identified at all. From stage 2 to stage 4 there was a slight further increase in Na and Pa latencies, with a more rounded Pa waveform. In deep, stage 4 sleep there was a dramatic reduction in amplitude of both Na and Pa.

Interestingly, in both of the wide-bandpass studies there was essentially no difference between the middle latency auditory evoked potentials recorded in REM sleep and those recorded during wakefulness. On the hypothesis that middle latency waves of the auditory evoked potential represent conscious awareness of the sound stimulus, this finding suggests that during REM sleep the subject is in some sense conscious of external sound stimuli, but that these conscious experiences may be incorporated into ongoing dreams rather than being interpreted in the normal waking context.

1.1 (i) (g) Auditory evoked potentials and selective attention

As discussed in Chapter 1, although the concept of attention is distinct from the concept of consciousness theoretically, in practical terms it is very difficult to separate the two. Some degree of attention to a stimulus is probably required for that stimulus to be consciously perceived. Thus if paying attention to a stimulus enhances a particular brain activity that is time-locked to the stimulus, this supports the hypothesis that the brain activity represents consciousness of the stimulus, but such support can not be regarded as unequivocal or conclusive, because the brain activity could also be a correlate of (a) the act of paying attention (b) a pre-conscious processing step or (c) processing at a higher level than simple sensory awareness (e.g. detection of difference or novelty, or activation of associations with some previous experience). Nevertheless, it is instructive to examine the brain-generated electromagnetic patterns that are affected by selective attention.

The effects of selective listening on scalp-recorded auditory evoked potentials have been studied extensively. Pioneering work by Hillyard's group (Hillyard, Hink, Schwent, & Picton, 1973) reported that the earliest segment of the auditory evoked potential that was increased when it was evoked by attended rather than unattended tones was the N1 wave. This difference between attended and unattended waveforms is variously known as the "N1 effect" (Hillyard, Hink, Schwent, & Picton, 1973), the "negative difference wave" or "Nd" (Hansen & Hillyard, 1980) and the "processing negativity" (Naatanen, Gaillard, & Mantysalo, 1978). It consists of at least two overlapping phases, the first of which has a scalp distribution similar to N1 itself and the second of which has a more frontal distribution and may last for hundreds of milliseconds (Giard, Perrin, Pernier, & Peronnet, 1988; Hansen & Hillyard, 1980). The "processing negativity", which has a partly frontal distribution, has been proposed as reflecting the degree of matching of a stimulus to an attentionally controlled template (Alho, Paavilainen, Reinikainen, Sams, & Naatanen, 1986; Alho, Sams, Paavilainen, & Naatanen, 1986; Naatanen, 1982). In terms of the model of attention sketched in Chapter 1, at least the frontal portion of this wave probably originates with the activity of neural generators of the process(es) of attention, rather than representing the effects of attention on conscious experience.

However, the conclusion that waves earlier than N1 were not affected by attention was revised when later work from the Hillyard group, using a task which required more highly focussed selective attention, showed that the middle latency waves between 20 and 50 ms after the stimulus were also altered by selective attention (Woldorff & Hillyard, 1991). These effects were paralleled by variations in target discrimination performance. MEG studies have also shown that neuromagnetic brain responses in the ranges 20–80 ms and 80–130 ms were increased in amplitude by selective attention (Woldorff, et al., 1993). The sources of these responses were reported to be in the auditory cortex, above the ears. This M20–50 effect was too small to be seen in individual subjects, but a grand-average approach allowed its generator to be localized 2–14 mm medial to the grand-average M100s and the individual M100s, on the supratemporal plane in, or slightly lateral to, Heschl's gyrus (i.e. in the primary auditory cortex). This location suggests that what we are seeing here may be the *effect* of an attentional process on the generator of sensation. Thus whatever attentional process is operating in this situation must itself be activated before the neural information reaches the primary sensory cortex. The scheme in Chapter 1 would suggest that such an attentional process may be mediated by the thalamic spotlight, which probably has the capacity to pre-regulate the responsiveness (i.e. the resting membrane potential) of whatever well-defined region of the primary auditory cortex responds to auditory stimuli of the frequency of interest. Thalamic activity itself is too deep in the brain to evoke a noticeable electric or magnetic field potential on the scalp, so all we see in EEGs or MEGs is its cortical effect.

In contrast to the situation just described, the frontal attention system is cortical and thus does evoke noticeable electric and magnetic evoked potentials. The mismatch negativity or MMN is a wave in the auditory evoked potential which peaks at 150–250 ms after a deviant sound in a repetitive sequence. Both MEG and EEG recordings show that this wave originates from a primary source in the auditory cortex and a secondary source in frontal cortex (Alho, 1995). Such a dual origin of the MMN in auditory and frontal cortices suggests that a template active in the prefrontal working memory area may be involved in deciding whether or not any given stimulus is different from those preceding it, and thus in generating the main MMN component in the auditory cortex. Early studies using low load selective attention tasks all showed that the MMN was not affected by selective attention. However again, a more recent study using a dichotic listening task which requires highly focussed attention to another sound source clearly demonstrates attentional modulation of the MMN generated in the auditory cortex (Woldorff, Hillyard, Gallen, Hampson, & Bloom, 1998).

In summary, a supportable hypothesis explaining the data above is that they reflect the actions of (at least) two attention systems, which have separate effects on the components of the auditory evoked potential. The proposed scenario is that the thalamic attention system primes certain areas of the primary auditory cortex (those which are activated by stimuli with the desired frequency characteristics) to be especially sensitive, thus generating a larger evoked response in the 20–80 ms post-stimulus range to attended stimuli. This represents an enhanced "raw" sensory experience of the stimuli to which attention is being paid. Then a booster system in the form of a frontal attention module cuts in at around 100 ms. This generates enhanced responses in the later auditory evoked potential range to stimuli which fit a certain expected template. The enhancement allows evoked responses to attended stimuli to be further processed more effectively than responses to non-attended stimuli, so that they can better be associated with past events or used as a trigger for future actions.

1.1(ii) (a) Auditory evoked potentials and deafness

The results concerning auditory evoked potentials and partial deafness are essentially the same as those previously described for sensation threshold. Both ABRs and MLRs have been used as predictors of sensation threshold, but MLRs give the more accurate predictions. Later waves are not good predictors of sensation threshold.

Total deafness is associated with a total lack of auditory evoked potentials. No results have been reported on the measurement of auditory evoked potentials for any "deaf-hearing" syndrome equivalent to "blindsight" (see Chapter 5).

1.2 Auditory evoked potentials covarying with subjective experience rather than properties of the physical stimulus

   (i) *Auditory evoked potentials and perceptual illusions*
   (a) *Pitch*

The human primary auditory cortex consists of Brodman areas 41 and 42, which are located within and around the lateral or Sylvian fissure, on the supratemporal plane of the transverse (Heschl) gyrus, just above the ear. In humans, as in all other species studied down to fish, it has been well demonstrated that the primary auditory cortex is tonotopically organized. This means that the spatial location of the neurons which best respond to particular sounds varies in a regular fashion according to the frequency of the sound.

Middle latency responses show such a tonotopic organisation in the primary auditory cortex, with the source of the Pam/Pa wave being progressively more superficial with higher stimulus frequencies (Pantev, et al., 1995). The site of generation of the brain electromagnetic event that occurs 100 ms after an auditory tone also varies in the auditory cortex as a function of the frequency of the tone (Pantev, et al., 1988; Romani, Williamson, & Kaufman, 1982), but the N1 tonotopic map is a mirror image of the middle latency map. The depth of the source of the N1m or N1 wave from the surface of the brain increases linearly with the logarithm of stimulus frequency, with higher frequency stimuli being associated with deeper N1m sources. This N1/N1m map lies several mm posterior to the Pa/Pam mirror map and it is controversial whether the N1m/N1 wave is due to activation of secondary auditory areas (Pantev, et al., 1995) or to a region of the primary auditory cortex (Yamamoto, Uemura, & Llinas, 1992). The post-stimulus latency of the maximal N1m also varies with stimulus frequency and intensity (Stufflebeam, Poeppel, Rowley, & Roberts, 1998).

N1 is associated with the detection of differences between the current stimulus and immediately preceding ones (Naatanen & Picton, 1987).

The mismatch negativity component of N1 arises from a neural change-detection system that compares the current stimulus to some kind of representation of whatever stimuli occurred within the previous 160 to 170 ms (Yabe, et al., 1998). So from the point of view of our argument, the logarithmic nature of the transform from tone frequencies to spatial location of N1 maxima perfectly fits with the logarithmic nature of Fechner's Law, the psychophysical law concerning ability of a subject to detect differences in pitch (see Appendix A).

The idea that this depth-related electromagnetic pattern is correlated with pitch (which is purely a subjective phenomenon) rather than stimulus frequency (which is an external physical property of the stimulus) is further reinforced by the results of another set of experiments, on a phenomenon known as the missing fundamental frequency (Pantev, Hoke, Lutkenhoner, & Lehnertz, 1991). If the auditory stimulus is a particular kind of complex tone in which the so-called fundamental frequency is missing, the subjective perception of a listener is that the pitch of the sound is that of the fundamental frequency (which is not actually present in the stimulus at all). In such a case, it turns out that perceived pitch is what determines the location of the MEG-detected dipole source, and not the actual spectral contents of the stimulus.

(b)   Sound localization

To localize the position of a sound source, animals use the cues of inter-aural differences in the intensity and time of arrival of sound waves in the air. Most of the detailed computation to allow this localization is done at sub-cortical levels, but the conscious perception of sound locality has been related to a particular auditory evoked potential (McEvoy, Picton, Champagne, Kellett, & Kelly, 1990). In order to elicit this potential, a continuous noise was generated by running a sequence of random numbers through a digital to analogue converter and playing the result through earphones. When two channels were programmed to generate identical noise stimuli but one channel was delayed relative to the other, the subject localized the sound to the side receiving the leading stimulus. Changes in the relative timing of the two stimuli caused the noise to shift in its lateralization. Since no difference could be detected in the ongoing monaural noise, any potentials evoked by these shifts were postulated to be specifically related to the binaural interaction. In this situation the scalp response recorded from the midline at the top of the head contained a positive-negative-positive complex with peak latencies of 75, 136 and 220 ms. This response was reported as being similar to that evoked by the onset of a monaural stimulus but smaller and significantly later.

In the early experiments referred to above no earlier evoked potential components could be elicited that were related to perceived lateralization shifts. However later experiments along similar lines but using MEG again implicated the neural events at around 30 ms after stimulus onset. P30m showed a tendency, similar to but smaller than that of N100m, to be larger to stimuli with contralaterally-leading inter-aural time differences (McEvoy, Makela, Hamalainen, & Hari, 1994). So far it has not possible to resolve any spatial patterns relating to conscious localization of sounds. Attempts to do so resulted in the statement that neurons in the human auditory cortex that were sensitive to interaural time differences were "not organized into a large-scale, orderly representation, which could be resolved by MEG" (McEvoy, Hari, Imada, & Sams, 1993).

(ii) Auditory evoked potentials and loudness

The amplitude of the MLR wave Pa increases as the stimulus intensity is turned up from 40 dB nHL to 70 dB nHL (Tucker & Ruth, 1996). This is consistent with the hypothesis that Pa is correlated with subjective sound sensation.

No clear correlation has been reported between the electrically measured N1 and perceived loudness: some subjects have an N1 that increases in amplitude with the stimulus intensity, whereas others have an N1 that saturates or becomes smaller at high stimulus intensity (Adler & Adler, 1989; Picton, Goodman, & Bryce, 1970). However, the N1–amplitude/stimulus-intensity slope is related to the amount of frontal midline theta activity in the general EEG, which in turn correlates with the degree of attention (Bruneau, Roux, Guerin, Garreau, & Lelord, 1993) and this does hint at a correlation between N1 amplitude and perceived loudness. Depth from the surface of the brain of the MEG-measured source of mN1 decreases with increasing stimulus intensity (the opposite of the case with increasing frequency) (Pantev, Hoke, Lutkenhoner, & Lehnertz, 1991), so there is some evidence for a pattern of correlation between the spatial features of N1 and loudness.

(iii) Auditory evoked potentials and perceptual changes due to learning

Tonotopic patterns in the primary auditory cortex do change with learning (Recanzone, Schreiner, & Merzenich, 1993). When owl monkeys were taught a frequency discrimination task, the size of the area in the primary auditory cortex that responded to the restricted frequency range in which the monkeys had learned to discriminate small differences was increased.

Relationship of global 40 Hz waves to auditory evoked potentials.

It has long been known that either steady state (Galambos, 1982; Galambos, Makeig, & Talmachoff, 1981) or transient (Pantev, et al., 1991) auditory stimulation elicits an oscillatory response at about 40 Hz. For some time there was an ongoing controversy about whether the 40 Hz steady state response that is generated by repetitive delivery of click stimuli at a frequency of 40 Hz was simply an algebraic addition of overlapping transient responses, or whether it represented the driving of an endogenous 40 Hz rhythm. Recently the evidence has been coming down on the side of the idea that there are endogenous 40 Hz rhythms in the brain, which can be reset or driven by sensory stimuli.

First, a new method of analysing MEG recordings called magnetic field tomography (Ribary, et al., 1991) showed that a 40 Hz oscillation is probably continuously generated by the brain, sweeping along the cortex from front to back once every 12.5 ms. The authors suggest that this oscillation can best be observed and averaged when it is reset and enhanced by sensory input. Secondly, convolution of the auditory stimulus-evoked MEG response by a Gabor wavelet (which gives a continuous measure of frequency-specific power over time) showed that there exist both a 40 Hz response which is not phase-locked to the discrete auditory stimulus provided and also one which is phase-locked to the stimulus (Tiitinen, Sinkkonen, May, & Naatanen, 1994). In these experiments the amplitude of the non-phase-locked 40-Hz waves was twice as high over the vision-related occipital cortex as it was over the auditory cortex (where the phase-locked activity was highest). This again suggests that there exists an endogenous 40-Hz oscillation, which may be "captured" locally by a particular sensory stimulus and become phase-locked to that stimulus.

The 40-Hz auditory evoked EEG response to transient stimulation is significantly larger when subjects pay attention to the stimulus than when they ignore it (Tiitinen, et al., 1993), which fits with the idea that it is the correlate of conscious awareness of the sound. However this response is insensitive to changes in qualitative stimulus features such as frequency (Tiitinen, Sinkkonen, May, & Naatanen, 1994). The latter observation can be explained in a number of ways. First, the 40-Hz response *per se* may have nothing to do with the contents of consciousness. I do not favor this explanation. Secondly, the methods so far used to measure and/or process the 40-Hz oscillation may not be sensitive enough to pick up stimulus-related frequency or amplitude modulations that do exist. This seems quite likely, considering that the temporal spreading introduced by the measurement method is enough to produce evoked waves that apparently begin before the onset of the stimulus (Tiitinen, et al., 1993)). Finally, pitch information may be represented by a spatial feature of the spatiotemporal electromagnetic pattern, rather than by a temporal feature. Evidence supporting the last possibility is given above, in the section on spatial patterns correlating with pitch perception.

Summary

It is clear that the 4–dimensional electromagnetic patterns we originally postulated to exist whenever auditory subjective experience exists have not yet been described in any detail. However there are significant indications that such patterns do exist, and we already have a great many useful pointers as to where and when to look for them. From the available evidence, we might predict that the spatiotemporal electromagnetic pattern which covaries with the raw sensation of sound is likely to be found covering the extent of the primary auditory cortex, at a time approximately 30 to 50 ms after a simple auditory stimulus. The pattern correlating with the subjective recognition that this sound is different from the sounds preceding it should be found covering the extent of the primary and possibly the secondary auditory cortices, from about 40 ms to about 250 ms after the stimulus. The pattern covarying with the subjective experience of any associations the sound evokes and consequent decisions as to what to do about the situation that gave rise to the sound is likely to be found about 300 ms after the stimulus, extending over a much wider extent of the cortex, taking in various association areas.

Thus, inasmuch as it is possible to isolate one auditory percept from the continuing stream of auditory consciousness, any particular percept must be considered as being a temporally smeared event which is probably continues to develop for up to about half a second after the stimulus. The spatial patterns in the electromagnetic field associated with the percept almost certainly change in time, spreading outwards from the primary auditory cortex until they eventually occupy virtually the entire cerebral cortex of the brain.

CHAPTER FIVE: VISION

❖ *Do there exist spatiotemporal configurations of the electromagnetic field that covary with visual consciousness?*

This chapter asks the question "does the brain generate patterns in the electromagnetic field that correlate with visual sensations?" By now we will be unsurprised to find that the answer is "yes."

Humans rely more on vision than on any other sense in negotiating their way around the world, so visual consciousness in humans is considerably richer in terms of information content than either olfactory or auditory consciousness. Thus it is not surprising that a much larger area of cortex is devoted to vision than to either of the other two sensory modalities. The cortex covering the entire back quarter of the brain is exclusively concerned with the processing of visual information and there are also extensive areas in several anterior regions that are important in vision. Therefore it might be expected that the spatiotemporal electromagnetic patterns we are looking for in the visual system would be much larger and more complex than those in either the olfactory or auditory systems.

Basic functional anatomy of the visual cortex

The exclusively visual regions of the cortex are subdivided into areas V1, V2, V3, V4, V5 and V6. Area V1 is the largest of these. It is situated at the back of the brain. V1 also has many other names, being known as either

(a) the striate cortex (because of its unique cytoarchitecture, which includes the "stripe of Gennari" in layer 4 where the input from the lateral geniculate nucleus enters the cortex) or

(b) the primary visual cortex (because it is the first cortical recipient of neural traffic from the eyes via the lateral geniculate nucleus[2]), or

(c) area 17 (because Korbinian Brodman, who subdivided the entire cortex into areas on the basis of cellular architecture, studied this area after the area he called 16 and before the area he called 18), or occasionally

(d) the calcarine cortex (because most of it is in or around the calcarine sulcus or fissure).

The other visual areas, V2 to V6, are collectively called the prestriate cortex, simply because they lie in front of (i.e. anterior to) the striate cortex. V1 projects axons to V2, and both V1 and V2 independently send direct connections to each of V3, V4, V5 and V6.

Functionally speaking, the visual system of mammals contains a number of separate topographic maps of the visual world. The visual field is first mapped in detail on the retina of the eye. This means that a neuron in any given position on the retina fires action potentials only in response to light in a particular position in the visual field. The retinal map is transferred through the lateral geniculate nucleus in a remarkably precise point-to-point fashion to V1 and thence with some modification to V2 and V3.

One principle we have already observed regarding the tonotopic maps in the auditory system is repeated in the visual system. This is that maps which are adjacent to one other in a flattened-out representation of the cortex tend to be mirror images of one another. For example, the topographic map in area V2 is a mirror image of the map in V1 and the map in V3 is a mirror image of the map in V2 (Zeki, 1993).

---

2   There is, however, a small projection from the lateral geniculate nucleus to the visual areas outside V1 (Fries, 1981; Yukie & Iwai, 1981). This is important in the interpretation of a type of "blindness" to be discussed later, in which the patient can discern visual information but has no conscious awareness of seeing (blindsight).

However in the visual system a new principle also becomes prominent. This is that the various different attributes of a stimulus (such as color, form and motion) are processed in parallel, in separate regions of the cortex (Zeki, 1978). Both areas V1 and V2 contain a wide variety of neurons: neurons that are selective for the motion of a visual stimulus, neurons that are selective for the orientation of the stimulus, neurons that are selective for wavelength of light and neurons that respond to 3–dimensional depth. The neurons that are selective for each of these sub-modalities of vision are certainly arranged in a precise retinotopic pattern within V1, but the point is that all the different sub-modalities are represented within area V1. They are all represented again in V2. However the other visual areas differ profoundly from each other in their functional properties.

For example, area V3 largely contains cells that respond only to a light-dark edge in the visual field. An individual neuron in V3 will only fire if there is a line or edge in its visual field that has a certain orientation in relation to the vertical. V3 is thus concerned with the perception of form. The angle of orientation of the line or edge to which a given V3 neuron responds changes gradually with the position of the neuron in V3, so that cells responsive to lines of similar orientation tend to be situated next to one another. This grouping together of cells that respond to similar features of the environment has been found to be a common feature of the organisation of all cortical areas. In terms of an overall spatial pattern which represents the stimulus, it fits with the idea that a particular region of the pattern represents a particular quality of the external stimulus evoking the pattern.

Area V4 is different from V3 in that it contains neurons that are responsive not to contrast, but to the wavelength of light impinging on their retinal field. Thus in the subjective sense, V4 is concerned with the processing of color. Cells in area V5 (a.k.a. MT) are specialised to respond only to a visual stimulus that is moving in a particular direction. Thus V5 is vital for the perception of motion. All of these findings were initially made in the macaque visual cortex, but later extended by the use of positron emission (PET) studies to the human visual cortex (Zeki, Watson, & Lueck, 1991).

In terms of our present hypothesis, that any given visual experience is identical with a particular spatiotemporal electromagnetic pattern, these data suggest that the patterns we are looking for will probably extend at least through areas V3 to V5 and will very possibly include V1 and the other visual areas as well. Furthermore, we can predict that the pattern correlating with a particular visual experience will extend across both hemispheres of the brain, to include the patterns generated by both left and right visual areas.

The suggestion that the patterns correlating with conscious experience will include elements generated in early visual areas such as V1 as well as later areas such as V4 and V5 goes directly against an old and well-entrenched notion which has had a major (albeit unspoken and perhaps unrecognised) influence on many current speculations about the neural correlates of consciousness. This is that the brain works in an exclusively hierarchical fashion. Grandmother cells (putative hypercomplex cells that respond only to an image of one's grandmother) are no longer as fashionable as they once were, but nevertheless some very eminent commentators have recently advanced the view that activity in the primary visual cortex does not enter consciousness (eg (Crick & Koch, 1995a; Crick & Koch, 1995b)). Some of the evidence presented in the following sections argues that this is not the case.

To return to the aim of this chapter, which is to examine critically the evidence already in the literature suggesting that the brain does generate electromagnetic patterns correlating with the contents of visual consciousness, only some of the criteria in Chapter 1 will be addressed here. These are 1.1(i)(h), 1.1(ii)(b) and 1.2(iii). There does exist a great deal of excellent experimental work on vision that is relevant to various of the other criteria in Chapter 1, and I would like to assure its authors that it is not left out of this discussion as a result of any desire on my part to offend them, but simply through a failure of energy and a feeling that enough evidence has already been adduced to make the point.

1.1 (i) (h): Spatiotemporal electromagnetic patterns varying with conscious perception during binocular rivalry

One criterion from Chapter 1 that has been the subject of a great deal of work by investigators interested in the neural correlates of visual consciousness is criterion *1.1(i)(h)*: "that any pattern claimed to correlate with visual experience should covary with conscious perception in the case of binocular rivalry".

The term binocular rivalry refers to a situation where each eye is presented with a different visual scene or pattern. When the information presented to each eye is different enough so that it cannot be fused into one binocular image, the two competing images are sometimes seen overlaid on top of one another, as might be expected, but it is also possible to adjust the stimulus parameters (brightness etc) so that each separate image is perceived alternately, with one percept spontaneously replacing the other every few seconds. This is termed a rivalrous situation. In terms of our current hypothesis, it is clear that any spatiotemporal electromagnetic patterns postulated to *be* (or even merely to be correlated with) visual consciousness must correlate with the dynamics of conscious perception in such a rivalrous situation. The patterns must change as the conscious percept changes. Have such patterns been found? The answer is almost, but not quite—there are tantalising pointers to the existence of electromagnetic patterns that obey this criterion, but the details are yet unclear.

Binocular rivalry has been investigated experimentally using both single cell recording methods in monkeys and cats, and electroencephalographic or neuromagnetic recordings in humans.

Binocular rivalry and single cell recordings

One major research program using single cell recordings to investigate binocular rivalry is that of Nikos Logothetis and colleagues. These investigators trained monkeys to press a particular lever on seeing a particular figure. They then recorded from cells in the monkeys' visual cortices, first during non-rivalrous conditions (when the same figure was presented to both of the monkey's eyes) and then during rivalrous conditions (when one figure was presented to one eye and another figure to the other eye). The experimenters characterised large numbers of neurons in non-rivalrous conditions and found that most cells responded best (i.e. fired most strongly) to one preferred figure. They then recorded the firing rates of the same neurons during rivalrous conditions and correlated these with which of the two figures the monkey reported seeing. The finding was that some neurons responded only when their preferred stimulus was perceived by the monkey, some responded best when it was suppressed and some neurons continued to respond to their preferred stimulus regardless of whether it was being perceived or not. Yet other neurons were relatively untuned during coherent, non-rivalrous stimulation but showed enhanced selectivity in response to rivalrous stimuli (Leopold & Logothetis, 1996; Logothetis & Schall, 1989; Sheinberg & Logothetis, 1997).

What is interesting in the present context is that the percentages of neurons in each of these classes depended on where in the cortex the neurons were. In areas V1/V2, V4 and V5, the majority of cells continued to respond to their preferred stimulus even when it was perceptually suppressed. In areas IT (the inferior temporal cortex) and STS (the upper and lower banks of the superior temporal sulcus) about 90% of the recorded cells reliably predicted the perceptual state of the animal, by firing only when their preferred stimulus was perceived. This result could be taken (and indeed has been taken, though not explicitly by the authors of the study) to mean that cells in V1 to V5 are not directly involved in whatever pattern of neuronal firing correlates with conscious perception, but are only involved in pre-conscious processing. However, it should be noted that 20% of the cells recorded from in V5 and 25% of cells in V4 did increase their firing rate significantly when their preferred stimulus was perceived, and a further 20% of neurons in V5 and 13% of neurons in V4 responded only when their preferred stimulus was phenomenally suppressed (Sheinberg & Logothetis, 1997). Thus a total of 40% of V5 neurons and 38% of V4 neurons did modulate their behavior in line with perception during binocular rivalry. About 18% of V1 cells behaved similarly. This indicates that any large-scale pattern of activity that correlates with conscious visual perception may receive contributions mainly from areas IT and STS, but probably also receives significant contributions from earlier visual areas as well. A further point to note is that there were no controls in these studies designed to remove the effects either of working memory or of preparation for the motor acts involved in reporting the monkey's perceptions (see Chapter 1). These contaminating factors must be considered more likely to influence the temporal areas IT and STS than the purely visual striate and prestriate cortex.

It should also be remembered that the simple fact that a particular neuron fires action potentials does not necessarily mean that it will contribute significantly to a large-scale pattern in the electromagnetic field. If what we are interested in is a spatial pattern in the electromagnetic field over an area of several cm², then it is important to recognise that neurons which fire in synchrony (i.e. coherently) will make a much larger contribution to such an electromagnetic pattern than neurons firing individually. The relative contribution to a field potential of coherently firing neurons (M) to incoherently firing neurons (N) has been estimated to be $M/\sqrt{N}$ (Elul, 1971). About 10^7 neurons line up in parallel within a 1 cm² portion of cortical gyrus. If only 1% are coherent, the relative contribution to scalp potential of these minority neurons would be approximately $10^5/\sqrt{10^7}$, or about 30 times greater than that of the 99% of neurons that produce incoherent sources (Nunez, 1995). Thus it becomes very important from the point of view of our current hypothesis to determine whether or not single neurons that follow perception also fire in synchrony with other neurons.

In fact the issue of synchrony of firing during binocular rivalry has been addressed, in a series of single cell experiments on cats. In early onset strabismus (squint), a binocular rivalry situation holds and signals conveyed by the two eyes are perceived not simultaneously but in alternation. Usually one eye becomes dominant and images presented to it are perceived most of the time. Wolf Singer's research group recorded from the primary visual cortex (V1) of awake strabismic cats, using moving stimuli and tracking which eye was doing the perceiving by measuring which eye controlled optokinetic nystagmus (a reflex which moves the perceiving eye in concert with the moving stimulus, in such a way as to keep the position of the image still on the retina) (Fries, Roelfsema, Engel, Konig, & Singer, 1997). As our present hypothesis would predict, neurons responding to the stimulus that was perceived fired with increased synchronicity. This means that their contribution to a large-scale spatiotemporal electromagnetic pattern would be significantly boosted. Conversely, neurons responding to the stimulus that was not perceived became less well synchronised, which would mean that their contribution to the relevant electromagnetic pattern would be minimised.

No changes in discharge rate were observed in this study, but it must be remembered that only neurons in V1 were examined and not neurons in areas V4, V5, IT or STS. The authors of the study simply say, "changes in synchronicity at early stages of processing are bound to result in changes of discharge rate at later stages"—meaning, presumably, that a barrage of synchronous excitatory postsynaptic potentials (epsps) would be likely to integrate and cause firing of their postsynaptic cells, whereas individually occurring epsps might not. This is of course another way of looking at the importance of synchronicity of firing. From the point of view of the current hypothesis though, the importance of synchrony is that cells firing synchronously will contribute much more to the overall spatiotemporal electromagnetic pattern than cells firing non-synchronously. Thus even a few synchronously firing cells in V1 could potentially contribute more to the overall electromagnetic pattern than a majority of cells in another area firing non-synchronously.

Clearly it would be useful to know the outcome, in either the cat or the monkey system, of experiments on correlation of perception with synchrony of firing in areas V4, V5, IT and STS (preferably with some controls included to eliminate the contribution of motor preparatory activity and working memory). However, it must be said that the sorts of large-scale spatiotemporal electromagnetic patterns we are looking for are probably not best studied using single-cell recording technology. It may turn out to be better to simply cut to the chase, by measuring the large-scale electromagnetic patterns directly, using the techniques of EEG and MEG.

Binocular rivalry and EEG/MEG in humans

The take-home message from a number of EEG and MEG studies on binocular rivalry is that the amplitude of the EEG or MEG response evoked by a visual stimulus is larger if the stimulus is perceived than if it is not.

One of the earliest EEG studies on binocular rivalry (Lansing, 1964) gave a particularly clear result in this regard. The experimenter presented to his subjects' left eyes a flickering light. This light evoked in the occipito-parietal EEG a rhythmic response of the same frequency as the flash rate of the light. At the same time he presented to his subjects' right eyes a steady red light with diagonal stripes. By varying the intensity of the red stimulus he could control whether it or the flickering light was perceived. The finding from this study was that the amplitude of the rhythmic EEG response to the flickering light closely corresponded with whether or not this stimulus was being perceived. When the flickering light was seen, the amplitude of the EEG response showed a marked increase. When it was not, the amplitude of the response dropped virtually to zero, even though the stimulus was physically still present at the same intensity.

Another early EEG study (MacKay, 1968) used the standard kind of averaged transient evoked potentials, taking advantage of two kinds of suppression phenomena that are slightly different from binocular rivalry. The first of these phenomena is termed "perceptual blanking". It involves simultaneous or close to simultaneous flash-presentation of a noise-patterned visual field (N) and a blank field (B) to the same eye. The outcome of this is that B suppresses perception of N if it is presented at the same time as, or up to 10 or 20 ms after N. However if B is presented at progressively longer intervals after N (eg 30, 40 and 50ms later), then its masking effect lessens and N becomes progressively more visible subjectively. The study found that as this happened, the characteristic EEG potential evoked by N appeared and progressively increased in amplitude. Thus there was again a correlation between evoked potential amplitude and subjective perception. The second suppression phenomenon is referred to as "interocular suppression" and involves presentation of N and B to different eyes. Under these conditions N suppresses B, even if presented several tens of ms after B. Again a correlation was found between subjective experience and evoked potential shape, at least for one pair of electrode placements in the occipital region.

Extension of Lansing's original work using a flickering light has led to the concept of frequency tagging of the stimuli presented to each eye, in order to derive an electrophysiological method suitable for measuring rivalry in real time. The so-called steady state visual evoked potential (SSVEP) evoked by a flickering grating follows the flicker frequency. As with Lansing's study, the amplitude of the SSVEP of a particular frequency has been found to depend on whether or not the stimulus of that frequency is being perceived (Brown & Norcia, 1997). The concept of frequency tagging was subsequently put to good use by Gerald Edelman's group, who employed it in conjunction with MEG recordings using a 148–sensor whole-head magnetometer (Srinivasan, Russell, Edelman, & Tononi, 1999; Tononi, Srinivasan, Russell, & Edelman, 1998). As with the EEG studies, the amount of MEG power at a particular frequency was found to depend on whether the stimulus which evoked that frequency of response was being perceived. In stimulus alternation trials a 100% modulation due to the physical presence/absence of the stimulus was observed. However during binocular rivalry this study found only a 50–85% decrease in power when the subject reported not being conscious of a particular stimulus. Thus some neural processing was still going on in the absence of conscious perception, but perception was clearly correlated with more intense spatiotemporal electromagnetic patterns.

Interestingly, this modulation by perceptual dominance, while not completely global, was distributed to a large subset of regions showing stimulus-related responses, including many anterior regions outside the visual cortex. In the words of the authors (Tononi, Srinivasan, Russell, & Edelman, 1998) "1. Neural responses to rivalrous visual stimuli occurred in a large number of cortical regions, both when the subject consciously perceived the stimuli and when he did not. 2. Responses evoked by a stimulus over a large portion of the scalp were stronger when the subjects were conscious of it than when they were not". Not only were frequency tagged responses stronger when a stimulus was perceived, but there was also a marked increase in both interhemispheric and intrahemispheric coherence at the stimulus frequency that was being perceived (Srinivasan, Russell, Edelman, & Tononi, 1999). The earlier mentioned analysis showing the disproportionately large contribution of coherently firing neurons to the overall electromagnetic pattern (Elul, 1971; Nunez, 1995) suggests that such an increase in coherence should actually be causally related to the increase in response amplitude. The fact that there was a correlation between perception and MEG field strength over the entire visual cortex—primary visual cortex, later visual areas and a number of other extra-visual areas—suggests that early visual areas are probably just as important in conscious perception as later visual areas (cf (Crick & Koch, 1995a)). The extra-visual areas which were actively correlated with perception may have been involved in working memory, attention and possibly with reporting of what was perceived.

1.1(ii) (b) Spatiotemporal electromagnetic patterns varying with conscious perception during neurological damage: blindsight

Despite its rarity, blindsight (Weiskrantz, 1997) is probably one of the most famous phenomena in the world of consciousness studies at the present time, so we will consider it briefly. Blindsight involves lesions to V1, which have the effect of destroying a subject's visual awareness or consciousness, while preserving some of their visual perceptual abilities. The patient thus maintains that they are blind in the part of their visual field which maps onto the site of the V1 lesion and strongly denies seeing anything in this area; but if forced to guess about stimuli presented to their blind hemifield they do significantly better than chance. There is a surprising lack of EEG studies of blindsight patients, but one which has been done (Shefrin, Goodin, & Aminoff, 1988) provides what could be seen as confirmatory evidence that some form of sensory processing is present, but without normal visual sensation. This study shows that a visually evoked P3 wave is present in response to stimuli in the blind hemifield, but earlier waves of the visual evoked potential such as P100 can only be elicited in the normally sighted hemifield.

On the face of it, this syndrome provides direct evidence that V1 is necessary for the generation of visual consciousness. When V1 is damaged, conscious visual experience is not available: some form stimulus-evoked sensation may enter awareness, but it is uniformly reported as being nothing like normal visual sensation. However, while V1 may be *necessary* for visual experience, a number of lesion studies over the years show that neither V1, nor any other specific area of visual cortex, is *sufficient* for normal visual experience (Weiskrantz, 1997).

This observation certainly fits with our present hypothesis, that the large-scale electromagnetic pattern generated by the whole visual cortex (and possibly some prefrontal areas as well) is the important thing. One prediction of the present hypothesis is that if any significant part of this large-scale pattern is destroyed, visual experience would be either compromised in a fairly predictable way (if the damage is in the more specialised visual areas concerned with eg color or motion) or would not occur at all (if the damage is to the striate cortex, where all features of vision are represented). As we have just pointed out, this prediction does seem to be supported by the evidence.

However the observation that damage to V1 causes a more serious effect on vision than damage to later areas does not necessarily mean that neurons in V1 contribute a more important feature of such a hypothetical overall pattern than do neurons in the pre-striate areas. It may be that one important feature generating the large-scale electromagnetic pattern is activity of the re-entrant connections between V1 and various pre-striate areas. Alternatively, it may simply be that lesions to V1 disrupt the main pathway for visual information from the periphery to the rest of the visual cortex, leaving only the relatively minor pathways that bypass V1(see footnote 2 at the beginning of this chapter). These bypass pathways may be able to support transfer of some information from the periphery to whatever site generates visual consciousness, but not that information which is actually important for conscious visual experience.

Basically, the critical experiments have not yet been done to determine what if any large-scale spatiotemporal electromagnetic patterns are present in the normal hemifields of blindsight patients and absent in their blind hemifields.

1.2 (iii) Spatiotemporal electromagnetic patterns varying with conscious perception not physical qualities of stimulus: learning

Again Walter Freeman's lab has reported seminal studies analogous to those on the olfactory and auditory systems, using arrays of subdural electrodes over the visual cortex of monkeys trained to respond to visual stimuli (Freeman & van Dijk, 1987). Two array positions were studied, one array covering Brodman areas 17, 18 and 19 and a smaller array covering only the primary visual cortex, with double the density of electrodes (at 0.6 cm separation compared to 1.2–1.4 cm separation in the larger array). Unfortunately no detailed analysis of differences between these two electrode arrays is presented, so no conclusions can be drawn as to whether patterns over the primary visual cortex correlate with perception better or worse than do larger scale patterns.

The behavioral task with which the EEG patterns were correlated was complex. The monkey had been trained to fixate on a square containing a checkerboard pattern that flickered at a reversal rate of 7.8 Hz. The onset of the flicker indicated that a trial was beginning. The flicker lasted for a time varying randomly between 1.5 and 5 seconds, after which it stopped and the monkey's prior training was to pull a lever between 400ms and 600ms later (in some trials between 300 ms and 500 ms) for a reward of apple juice. Trials were repeated every 4–6 seconds, while a larger checkerboard in a different area of the screen was flicked on for 340 ms and off for 500ms continually, without reward contingency. Four different epochs were differentiated, each assumed to be associated with a different behavioral state:

(1) the first 100 ms after cessation of the flicker (the averaged visual evoked potential to the cessation of the flicker was reported to be longer than 100 ms but shorter than 200 ms)

(2) the period from 200 ms to 400 ms after cessation of the flicker (this was "associated with the CS (conditioned stimulus) onset"—i.e. , if the monkey was concentrating on the task, he was deciding to pull the lever during this period)

(3) the period from 400 to 600 ms after cessation of the flicker (associated with the CR (conditioned response)—the monkey was pulling the lever and looking at the mouthpiece)

(4) the period from 600 to 800 ms after cessation of the flicker (associated with the UCS (unconditioned stimulus)—the monkey was drinking his juice, if he had responded correctly).

Within each of these epochs, shorter time segments were selected by eye in which the EEG showed bursts of high amplitude oscillations lasting 75–200 ms, during which there was high coherency across channels. It is argued that "this basic structural coherence was not due to a contribution from the reference electrode because the amplitude differed between channels". Superimposed on this widespread coherence (in which the EEG power was distributed in a form resembling "1/f noise"—in other words there was more power at lower frequencies) were shorter localized episodes of coherence in which the power was concentrated into a single or at most two peaks at frequencies between 20 and 40 Hz. These peaks were variable in different trials.

When a Principal Components Analysis was applied to data from the burst periods, a waveform common to all channels could be extracted, that incorporated most of the total variance. The distribution of the power of this component across electrodes gave a spatial pattern of the coherent activity and statistical analyses suggested that different such patterns were associated with the CS and the CR periods (when the monkey was looking at and pulling the lever and when he was looking at the mouthpiece and receiving his reward). These patterns remained stable over 6 weeks. As with the olfactory system, patterns that differentiated CS and CR could only be extracted after a form of channel normalization was applied, to remove a basic spatial pattern of power distribution which probably reflects the relationship between individual anatomy and electrode placement.

This particular series of experiments used only one monkey and no new learning was studied. But in general, the results repeat the findings of similar experiments on the olfactory and auditory systems (see Chapters 3 and 4), where spatiotemporal electromagnetic patterns were found to correlate not with a stimulus *per se*, but with the meaning the stimulus had for the animal. The electromagnetic patterns thus changed when learning gave a particular stimulus a new meaning and the stimulus came to be perceived differently. In other words, these electromagnetic patterns correlated with the conscious perception of a stimulus, not with its physical qualities. Unfortunately at this stage the published data do not allow a useful qualitative description of what the patterns look like and how constant they are between individuals for a given external stimulus—but statistically the patterns do predict the perceptual state of the animal, as far as can be determined.

Summary

Again we do not have detailed information on the characteristics of the 4–D electromagnetic patterns that covary with visual consciousness, but we do have significant indications that such patterns exist. While some of the available evidence on the visual system has been interpreted by some commentators as showing that only neural activity in relatively restricted areas of cortex is the neural correlate of visual consciousness, my own view is that the spatial electromagnetic pattern over the entire visual cortex will turn out to be the defining feature of visual experience. Thus it may be predicted that the size and complexity this pattern will make vision a much more difficult modality to study in terms of the architecture of consciousness than hearing, despite the fact that more is currently known about the neurophysiology of vision than of audition. However in order to abstract the important features of the spatiotemporal electromagnetic patterns defining consciousness, it will obviously be necessary to study several sensory modalities in parallel, so that their characteristic electromagnetic patterns can be compared and contrasted.

CHAPTER SIX: THE ELECTROMAGNETIC FIELD THEORY OF CONSCIOUSNESS

- ❖ *Expanded statement of theory*
- ❖ *Why not all brain activity is conscious*
- ❖ *The binding problem*
- ❖ *Electromagnetic field theory and psychoneural identity theory*
- ❖ *Practical consequences*
- ❖ *Positive evidence for the theory*

The experimental evidence presented in chapters 2 to 5 has basically confirmed our initial hypothesis that both states and contents of consciousness do covary with certain spatiotemporal configurations of the electromagnetic field. This makes it worthwhile to generate and examine a slightly more fleshed-out version of the electromagnetic field theory of consciousness.

We may begin by restating the basic tenet of the theory, which is that conscious experience is a fundamental property of certain configurations of the electromagnetic field.

It is important to note that the word fundamental is here taken as meaning "not able to be reduced or explained in terms of anything simpler"—there is no implication that a fundamental property of the electromagnetic field is a uniform property of the field. The present proposal specifically does not imply that all parts of the electromagnetic field are conscious at all times, which would entail some form of panpsychism. Rather, it is proposed that consciousness, like light and matter, is non-uniformly distributed in space and time. In one sense, since various spots in the field are conscious at various times, the field as a whole can be regarded as having the property of consciousness (in the same way as a cloth with red spots on it can be regarded as having the property of redness). However in another and very important sense, consciousness is localized. A given spatial location in the field can be magnificently conscious at some times, partially conscious at other times and not conscious at all for most of the time. In other words, the hypothesis allows for the ability of consciousness to move about in space with its biological associates and to fluctuate in intensity, as in different levels of anesthesia or sleep.

The electromagnetic field theory of consciousness also allows for the existence of different types of consciousness. The consciousness of humans probably differs from the consciousness of that famous philosopher's familiar the bat, for example (Nagel, 1974) and the present theory in principle explains why: because the spatiotemporal electromagnetic field-configurations generated by bat brains differ from those generated by human brains. Likewise, the different qualia experienced by any particular human subject are different: hearing is different from vision and both are different from smell. The electromagnetic field theory of consciousness predicts or explains this also: the spatiotemporal electromagnetic field configurations generated by the auditory cortex differ from those generated by the visual cortex and the field configurations generated by the olfactory system differ from both. Different sensory experiences within one sensory modality also differ. For example, the experience of hearing a 500 Hz sound differs from the experience of hearing a 1000 Hz sound. The theory explains this as being due to the fact that the spatial electromagnetic field configuration generated by the auditory cortex in response to a 500 Hz pressure wave in the ambient air is different from that generated in response to a 1000 Hz wave. The reader will have noticed that all of these statements about how the theory explains various differences in consciousness concern measurable differences in the spatiotemporal electromagnetic field configurations that are generated by brains in various situations. They are all supported by extensive existing empirical evidence, as documented in Chapters 3 to 5 of this book (except, it must be admitted, the part about the bat—there do exist extensive data on the field-configurations generated by bat brains, but in the interests of brevity I have chosen not to document them here).

Why not all brain activity is conscious

One previously intractable question which is easily answered by the electromagnetic field theory of consciousness is why only some of the neural activity that goes on in brains enters consciousness. On the present theory we are not required to postulate that some specialised neurons possess a kind of magical consciousness-stuff that has so far not been identified, which seems to be the onay out of the dilemma if one concentrates on single neurons. The explanation offered by the present theory is simply that only some configurations of the electromagnetic field have the property of consciousness. The important thing is not individual neurons, but the spatiotemporal pattern of neural firing over large groups of neurons, which does generate a conscious field-configuration in some circumstances and does not in others. At this stage the precise spatiotemporal features that are the signature of a conscious, as opposed to an unconscious field-configuration are still to be determined, but this question would appear to be eminently accessible experimentally.

The binding problem

Another previously knotty problem which is essentially dissolved by the electromagnetic field theory of consciousness is the question of why conscious experience has an apparent unity to it. We know that when we perceive a visual scene for example, the neurons that fire in response to various aspects of the scene (color, movement, form) are located in fairly widely separated areas of the brain. Yet our overall perception of the scene seems to occur all at once, in a completely integrated way. In fact on the basis of its Latin derivation, the word consciousness can be taken as *meaning* "knowing things together" or "all at once". This feature of consciousness has in the past been baffling because it has been implicitly assumed that there must be a single place in the brain where all information has to converge in order to give rise to a conscious experience. The fact that it would take a finite amount of time for information to get to this hypothetical place from all the various regions of the brain where it was constructed is thus upsetting and has led to the proposal of various rather uncomfortable solutions. Several commentators have even suggested that quantum non-locality must have something to do with mind, although they are generally not very specific about what (Hodgson, 1991).

On the electromagnetic field theory of consciousness, however, no such extreme solutions are necessary. The visual experience of any given moment in time is simply the whole pattern in the electromagnetic field that exists as a result the activity of all the parts of the brain occupied with processing vision at that moment. On this interpretation, one spatial part of the electromagnetic pattern in the brain is the conscious experience of the color red occupying a particular region of space in the world, another spatial part of the electromagnetic pattern in the brain is the conscious experience of a balloon-shaped object occupying the same region of space in the world and a third spatial pattern in the brain is the experience of movement in that region of space in the world. When all of these parts of the electromagnetic pattern in the brain are present at a particular moment in time, the conscious perception of the moment is that a red balloon is floating through that part of the world. If the movement part of the pattern is missing, the balloon stays still. If the red part of the pattern changes to a yellow pattern, the balloon changes color. And so on.

So on this theory, the conscious mind of an individual is the sum total of all the conscious field-configurations that are spatially coincident with the individual's brain. Any conscious field-configurations existing in your brain at a given moment are automatically part of your experience at that moment. The binding problem simply does not arise.

For the present articulation of the electromagnetic field theory of consciousness then, there is no "binding problem". The only problem is working out from empirical observations exactly what rules relate various parts of the brain-generated electromagnetic pattern to various factors in the perceptual experience. This is by no means a trivial problem technically, but it is at least a relatively easy one conceptually.

The electromagnetic field theory of consciousness and the psychoneural identity theory

The theory about the nature of consciousness which has probably always been held (though never spoken) by the majority of working cellular neuroscientists has most recently been articulated by Francis Crick, in his book The Astonishing Hypothesis (Crick, 1994). As Crick puts it:

> "The Astonishing Hypothesis is that "You", your joys and your sorrows, your memories and your ambitions, your sense of personal identity and free will, are in fact no more than the behavior of a vast assembly of nerve cells and their associated molecules. As Lewis Carroll's Alice might have phrased it: "You're nothing but a pack of neurons."

In fact this hypothesis has been around in print for at least 30 years (Fiegl, 1967) and the conceptual difficulties that make it astonishing were well discussed by Gordon Globus a little over 25 years ago (Globus, 1973). The idea is generally known as the psychoneural identity theory, because it essentially holds that consciousness is identical with the firing of neurons.

The electromagnetic field theory of consciousness has some similarities with the psychoneural identity theory, in that the electromagnetic patterns postulated to be identical with consciousness in the electromagnetic field theory are at present only generated by the coordinated firing of neurons. However the two theories are sharply differentiated by one obvious feature. This is that, if we knew enough about the spatiotemporal characteristics of the field-patterns proposed by the present theory to be conscious, it would in principle be possible to generate them in the total absence of neurons.

This suggests an obvious experimental test of the present theory. If we could describe in enough detail the spatial electromagnetic pattern that covaries with the sound of middle C, for example, we could in principle use hardware (instead of wetware) to generate a little lump of middle-C-experience in one corner of the room. The difficulty with this test would of course be deciding whether the field patterns so generated were indeed conscious, since they would exist in total isolation and would not have the benefit of being associated with a language or other behavioral system that would allow either reportage of or inference about their subjective character. Even if they could be provided with such a system, the entity in question would be likely to encounter the sort of speciesist prejudice that initially bothered the fictional Mr Data of Star Trek fame—some possessors of a wetware brain would simply refuse to believe the report of a hardware-instantiated being concerning its private subjective experiences.

However this problem of verifying the subjective quality of an artificial middle-C quale might conceivably be overcome by the positioning of a biological brain in the same location as the artificially generated electromagnetic patterns. It is a reasonable prediction that the artificial conscious experience might then be integrated into the consciousness generated by the biological brain and thus experienced by the "I" associated with that brain. Success of this prediction would have a number of consequences that could turn out to be of some importance for human society.

Practical consequences of the electromagnetic field theory of consciousness

1.   One consequence of successful generation of conscious field-configurations in the absence of biological neurons is that genuinely conscious computers could become a reality. The hardware of such entities would have to be organized along entirely different lines from that of the current generation of computers, because in order to generate conscious experiences it would have to generate complex spatiotemporal electromagnetic patterns, rather than linear strings of digital bits and bytes. But in principle these entities could eventually possess all of the relevant characteristics that define a human person. Therefore ethically, they would have to be granted similar rights to humans. This would no

doubt include the right not to be turned off. Such beings would have one characteristic that would distinguish them from humans however and that is the potential for what would be essentially immortality. Human bodies wear out after a mere century or so, but silicon (or whatever material is eventually used) can keep its configuration for thousands of years. So these conscious beings would have the potential to become immensely old and wise. They would also have the potential to possess senses that humans do not have. In principle their makers could copy the senses of sonar-using species such as bats and dolphins, or could provide the ability for their creations to navigate by detecting magnetic variations like pigeons or to detect minute levels of chemicals in the environment like insects. Completely new kinds of sensory consciousness could also be invented, capable of detecting environmental radiation outside the light range. Creatures possessing such characteristics would certainly make interesting friends and acquaintances.

2.   A second consequence which would follow from the successful generation of conscious experiences in the absence of neurons would be a complete reconstruction of the education and entertainment industries. If it did turn out to be possible to generate a little disembodied lump of conscious experience in the air and have it integrate it into a biological consciousness simply by placing the head in the right place in the field, then movies as we know them would rapidly become so old-hat as to be merely a historical curiosity. They would be replaced by complete experiences, including not just sight and sound but all the other sensory modalities and emotions as well. Virtual reality would be an order of magnitude more real than it currently is. Learning could become completely experiential, virtual tourism might relieve summer congestion at the world's beauty spots and the present illicit pharmaceuticals industry would no doubt find itself seriously undermined.

3.   A third practical consequence of the ability to generate conscious experiences non-biologically and have these integrate into a biological consciousness would be the possibility of generating artificial sensory

experience for the blind or deaf, for example. It might also be possible to generate inverse electromagnetic field configurations to cancel out unwanted biologically-generated experiences like chronic pain.

In short, if this theory and its predictions turn out to be right, we are looking at nothing less than a major revolution in the way we live.

Evidence for the electromagnetic field theory of consciousness

But will the theory and its predictions turn out to be right? The only way to find out for sure is to measure some sensory patterns, generate them artificially and shove someone's head into the artificial patterns. However before we go to such a considerable amount of trouble, we can certainly take a further look at the current situation with regard to the verifiability of the theory.

According to Popper, it is not possible to prove a scientific theory—the best that can be done is to fail to disprove it. The failure of some attempts to disprove the present theory will be described in Chapter 8. However, whatever the excellence of Popper's dictum in a logical sense, the sociology of science dictates that what actually causes a theory eventually to be accepted is not repeated failure to disprove it, but the existence of a large body of positive evidence supporting it. Positive evidence that so far exists to support the electromagnetic field theory of consciousness can be summarised as follows:

(a) There do exist spatiotemporal patterns in the electromagnetic field that covary with states of consciousness. Empirical evidence for this is detailed in Chapter 2.

(b) There do exist spatiotemporal patterns in the electromagnetic field that covary with the contents of consciousness, in at least three sensory modalities. Some of the empirical evidence for this in the modalities of olfaction, audition and vision is detailed in Chapters 3, 4 and 5.

(c) Spatiotemporal patterns in the electromagnetic field similar to those proposed as being conscious not only can, but on a routine basis do affect brain function. Thus the electromagnetic field theory not only shows how brains generate consciousness, but also provides a mechanism by which consciousness can have a causal effect in the brain that generated it. Empirical evidence for this is presented in the following chapter.

CHAPTER SEVEN: FIELD EFFECTS AND MIND-BRAIN INTERACTION

- *Mind-brain interactions*
- *History of the idea that electromagnetic fields influence the brain*
- *Empirical evidence that electric fields are important in brain function*
- *Field effects and the uses of consciousness*
- *Mind-brain interactions*

Common sense notions of how the world works suggest that a conscious decision to move a finger can be the efficient cause of finger movement. If we accept this, then we must accept that mental events can cause the firing of action potentials in the brain (and therefore in peripheral nerves and finally muscles). In other words, unless we are prepared to relegate our own consciousness to the status of a secondary epiphenomenon, which merely fools us into thinking that it affects our actions but which actually has neither causal powers nor any use at all, then we must accept that an individual mind does have the ability to move matter in its own brain. Philosophers may play with zombies and neurophysiologists may operate professionally on the assumption that consciousness is merely an epiphenomenon, but few of us are on a day-to-day level willing to give up the notion that we (i.e. our conscious minds) can exert an influence on what we do. Therefore one major requirement of a satisfying theory of consciousness must be that it should be obvious how whatever the theory proposes as being identical with consciousness can influence the physiological function of the brain.

This fairly basic requirement generally defeats dualist theories of consciousness, which argue that mind and matter are fundamentally different and thus that consciousness is non-physical. Quantum mechanical speculations notwithstanding, it is not at all obvious from our present understanding of physics how a purely non-physical entity or event could directly cause the rearrangement of matter that underlies the firing of even a single neural action potential. The requirement also causes serious problems for purely materialist accounts of consciousness such as the psychoneural identity theory. On this idea, consciousness *per se* can not have any causal properties, because consciousness is just what-the-brain-does and the brain, being a material instrument, simply carries out its appointed tasks in a purely mechanical way according to the deterministic principles of cause and effect. The "self" (which must be simply another brain process) then either does or does not become aware of the outcome of the other deterministic processes that produce behavior. In other words, according to the neural identity theory, our view of ourselves as having "free will" or being able to make conscious choices must be purely an illusion. While it is not impossible that an idea so counterintuitive could be correct, it would certainly be more comfortable to encounter a theory which did allow for conscious decisions to have some causal efficacy.

The theory being put forward here does allow for consciousness to have causal efficacy. While not frankly dualist, it is not materialist in the usually accepted sense either. To reiterate, the present theory is that consciousness is identical with certain spatiotemporal patterns in the electromagnetic field. Although they are not matter exactly, these electromagnetic patterns are physical in the sense that they are readily able to exert a back-influence on the physiology of neurons in the brain which generated them. In fact the evidence that such electromagnetic patterns do influence neuronal physiology is clear and present and does no violence at all to currently accepted notions of how the physical world works. So on the electromagnetic field theory of consciousness, there is no in-principle objection to the idea that consciousness *per se* can have a direct effect on the behavior of the organism.

This chapter starts by describing the fluctuating history of the idea that brain-generated electromagnetic fields are important in the normal function of the brain and then details more recent evidence that the sorts of electromagnetic patterns we are proposing as being identical with consciousness do routinely influence brain physiology on a millisecond to millisecond basis. For a full appreciation of this evidence, the reader should be familiar with the material presented in Appendix B, on the currently accepted basics of cellular neurophysiology and also that in Appendix C, on how these cellular mechanisms operate in the generation of what are today called field potentials.

History of the idea that electromagnetic fields influence the brain

(a) Kohler v Lashley

The idea that endogenous electric fields are important in normal brain function probably first emerged in the Gestalt psychology of Wolfgang Kohler in the 1920s (Kohler, 1920; Kohler, 1929). Kohler's theory, much of which was originally published in German, is summarized in a review by Karl Lashley (Lashley & Semmes, 1951). To use Lashley's words, Kohler's field theory was "based on the following assumptions:

1. There is a topological projection of the sensory surfaces upon the cerebral cortex and the distribution of afferent excitations corresponds to the spatial pattern of sensory stimulation.

2. Nerve impulses, relayed to the cortex, generate local differences in potential, probably by liberation and local accumulation of some chemical (Kohler, 1940) p75f.

3. The electromotive force developed in the cortex is proportional to the number of afferent impulses reaching that point in unit time (Kohler, 1940) p75f.

4. The differences in potential result in a pattern of flow of current, the density of current at any point depending upon the E.M.F. developed at that point, the potential of all other points in the system and the relative conductivity of all parts of the conducting system within which it lies.

5. Subject to certain qualifications, the nervous tissue is homogeneous in respect to the conduction of current (Kohler, 1920)p236 ff.

6. The flow of current is "relational"; any local change in potential or resistance alters the pattern of flow throughout the entire field.

7. The field of distribution of effective current flow is molar; that is, the cortical area within which the relational pattern of current develops is at least of the magnitude of the sensory image as projected to the cortex and may, in fact, include the whole brain. (A visual object subtending 12 degrees on the central retina would, for example, produce a "figure-field" of high potential covering some 2 sq. cm. on each occipital lobe of the rhesus monkey, with a surrounding flow throughout a larger area.)

8. With flow of current, a polarization of membranes in the tissue occurs, with consequent change in the pattern of current flow. There is also a progressive change in polarizability with continued flow of current (electrotonus). This is the basis of explanation of compensation for distortion in cortical projection and for figural after-effects (Kohler & Wallach, 1944).

9. In a later formulation (Kohler & Wallach, 1944) it is suggested, following Gerard and Libet (Gerard & Libet, 1940), that the cortex may act as a polarized layer. In such case current flow would presumably depend upon local depolarization of the layer, but this possibility is not discussed in any detail.

10. The characteristics of perceptual organization correspond to the distribution of current within the cortical receptive area. A dense, continuous current flow apparently constitutes a figure (figure-current) and an interruption of flow or sharp gradient of intensity, a contour or interruption of figure (Kohler, 1938) p217. The apparent distance of separation of objects in vision is assumed to correspond to the degree of "functional relationship" established by current flow. Kohler and Wallach refrain from defining this functional relationship precisely (Kohler & Wallach, 1944) p 334), but since increase in apparent distance in figural after-effects is accounted for on the basis of development of electrotonus (Kohler & Wallach, 1944) p 329, the closeness of functional relationship is presumably in inverse relationship to the resistance of the tissue."

This theory of Kohler's was remarkably prescient in many respects and was quite influential among psychologists of the day—until it ran into Lashley. Lashley performed what he saw as an experimental test of Kohler's ideas, as follows. In one monkey he placed four thin strips of gold foil under the dura along the surface of the visual cortex. In one more monkey he inserted a number of gold pins into the visual cortex at right angles to the surface. The aim of these manipulations was to short-circuit electric current flow in the cortex, thus distorting the postulated "figure-currents" and therefore (if the theory was correct) distorting visual perception. However Lashley made no attempt to determine whether there was in fact any disruption of current flow induced by his gold strips or inserts.

To examine the effects of the gold inserts on visual perception, Lashley tested the monkeys once, as soon as they recovered from the anesthetic. He used four visual discrimination tasks, on which the monkeys had been trained before the operation. The tasks were to choose one of two metal plates covering food dishes: in the first task they had to discriminate between a red and a green plate, in the second between a striped plate and a plate with a diamond on it, in the third between an "S" and a cross and in the fourth between dots in a diamond shape and random dots. The monkeys performed about as well after the operation as they had before, both on these tests and on tests like locating and retrieving bits of food that were in plain view (except that it was noted that the one with inserted pins "occasionally failed to see a small bit of food in the cup"). On the basis of this, Lashley felt justified in concluding that "the action of electric currents, as postulated by field theory, is not an important factor in cerebral integration" (Lashley & Semmes, 1951).

By today's standards, it is probably fair to say that the paper reporting these experiments would never have made it past the referees of any reputable journal. Lashley reports no attempts to measure whether the pins or strips did in fact produce any of the "significant distortions of the electrical field" which they were assumed to have produced. The monkeys were tested only once. He reports no attempts to follow up the small behavioral change, suggestive of at least a minor distortion of vision, that was noted in the monkey with inserted pins. In fact the quality of these experiments is reminiscent of what must have been the quality of experimentation that led Lashley to state unequivocally in 1948 that "Uncomplicated destruction of major portions of the prestriate region...has not been found to produce any disturbances in sensory or perceptual organization (Lashley as quoted in (Mishkin, Ungerleider, & Macko, 1983)). In this latter instance it is difficult to know whether it was a preconceived idea that the neural tissue of the brain is functionally homogeneous that led to inadequate experimentation, or badly done experiments that produced the idea that the brain is functionally homogeneous, but Lashley was certainly convinced of this idea (Lashley, 1950). The notion that brain tissue is functionally homogeneous has of course been shown subsequently to be completely wrong, as a cursory glance at any basic neuroscience text written in the last thirty years will show. Lashley's conclusion that electric field effects are not important in the brain is similarly wrong, as shown by work quoted later in this chapter.

Whatever the quality of his experimentation however, Lashley was (and to some extent still is) an extremely influential investigator. Also, his conclusions about the irrelevance of electric field effects in brain function fitted in general with the independent ideas concurrently being arrived at by Jack Eccles, who was just as influential among physiologists as Lashley was among psychologists.

(b)   Eccles v Eccles

During the 1930s an ongoing debate raged between pharmacologists (led by Sir Henry Dale) and physiologists (led by Sir John Eccles) about whether neurons communicate by means of chemical or electrical transmission. At the time, the only verified example of chemical transmission known was vagal inhibition of the heart. This inhibition seemed to operate so slowly that physiologists in general and Eccles in particular preferred the idea that the faster communication known to occur at other synapses must be mediated directly by the electrical currents associated with action potentials. However when Eccles' own pioneering intracellular recordings in the central nervous system clearly showed that at least some central synaptic transmission actually is chemical (and when Sir Karl Popper had sat Sir John Eccles down and convinced him that in science it is not only acceptable but actually honorable to disprove one's own hypotheses), this strong preference for electrical transmission was swiftly and properly abandoned (Brock, Coombs, & Eccles, 1952). Unfortunately the pendulum of the *zeitgeist* then swung completely against any importance of intercellular electrical effects in the brain at all. Not only direct neuron-to-neuron electrical transmission (which we now know actually does sometimes occur) but also the idea that electric fields operating at larger distances might be important were forgotten in the new enthusiasm for chemical transmission. In the minds of most neuroscientists, the baby was, at least temporarily, thrown out with the bathwater.

Evidence that electric fields actually are important in normal brain function

After these two body blows, the idea that electric fields are important in brain function lay dormant for some years. But you can't keep a good idea down and experimental results soon started quietly accumulating to support the notion.

(a) Field effects and the Mauthner cell

In the 1960s and 70s, work on the Mauthner cell in the medulla of the goldfish (Faber & Korn, 1973; Furshpan & Furukawa, 1962; Furukawa & Furshpan, 1963; Korn & Faber, 1975) showed that under normal conditions, a positive extracellular current generated by a group of interneurons produces a functional inhibition of the M-cell, hyperpolarizing its axon hillock and initial segment and thus preventing it from generating action potentials. One special condition favoring this particular example of an electric field effect in the central nervous system is that the extracellular resistance in this region is about five times higher than that of adjacent tissue (see Appendix C for an explanation of why this increases the size and effectiveness of extracellular field potentials). This high resistance is due to the fact that the axon hillock, initial axon segment and portions of the soma of the M-cell are surrounded by a so-called axon cap, which is penetrated by the terminals of the interneurons. The terminals of the interneurons do also make inhibitory chemical synapses with the M-cell (which confirms the suggestion that single neurons may mediate both electrical and chemical inhibition of their target cell), but these terminals do not have any electrotonic contacts (gap junctions) with the M-cell. This is an important point. Field effects involve coupling through the extracellular space, not via specialised low-resistance junctions.

In the case of the Mauthner cell, a reciprocal field effect of the M-cell on the interneurons has also been demonstrated (Korn & Faber, 1973). When the M-cell is active, it also effects a field effect inhibition of the interneurons. As well as the high extracellular resistance in the area, a second condition favoring the occurrence of this field effect is that the processes of the interneurons lie in parallel with the lines of extracellular current flow associated with the M-cell action potential (Faber & Korn, 1989). This arrangement favors the intracellular channeling of current and thus the occurrence of field effects.

(b)   Field effects and the cerebellum

Another structure in the central nervous system with the same encapsulated geometry as the M-cell is the mammalian cerebellar cortex. Here the axon terminals of basket cells converge on and surround the initial segment of the Purkinje cells (Palay & Chan-Palay, 1974). The orderly arrangement of Purkinje cells also establishes them as likely targets for field effects, particularly in the presence of radially directed extracellular currents. Thus it is not too surprising that electrical inhibition of the Purkinje cells has been demonstrated (Korn & Axelrad, 1980). Again as with the M-cell, the inhibitory basket cells mediate a two-component inhibition of their target Purkinje cells, with an early electrical phase being succeeded by a later classic chemical ipsp (inhibitory postsynaptic potential).

(c)   Field effects and the hippocampus

Another structure where relatively high extracellular resistances occur is the hippocampus. In rat hippocampus, resistivity measurements show an extracellular impedance 1.5–3 times higher around the pyramidal and granule cell bodies than in intermediate regions, for reasons that are not clear (Jefferys, 1984). Again pyramidal and granule cells are lined up in a conspicuously orderly fashion. On the basis of these two conditions, it might be expected that extracellular fields would influence pyramidal and granule cell physiology in the hippocampus and in fact such a finding has now been demonstrated by a number of studies. Extracellular electric fields generated by the activity of nearby neurons have been shown to influence pyramidal cell excitability and synchronization under normal conditions in the dentate gyrus of the rat hippocampus *in vitro* (Snow &

Dudek, 1986) and also in rat hippocampal regions CA1 and CA3 both *in vitro* (Richardson, Turner, & Miller, 1984; Snow & Dudek, 1986; Turner, Richardson, & Miller, 1984) and *in situ* (Dalkara, Krnjevic, Ropert, & Yim, 1986; Taylor, Krnjevic, & Ropert, 1984; Yim, Krnjevic, & Dalkara, 1986). These electric field effects are associated with population spikes[3] in neighboring cell populations and act by inducing subthreshold passive depolarizations of the cell bodies of nearby pyramidal cells, which can be demonstrated in the complete absence of chemical synaptic transmission. These subthreshold depolarizations have the effect of exciting and synchronizing the population of pyramidal cells.

(d) Field effects and the cerebral cortex

A number of regions of the cerebral cortex obviously fulfil at least one of the requirements for the effectiveness of electric field effects, in that neurons there are arranged in an orderly, lined-up fashion. However no studies have been reported on extracellular resistivity measurements in various regions of the cerebral cortex and no studies comparable to those done on the hippocampus have been done to see whether field effects are significant under normal conditions in the cerebral cortex.

Field effects and the uses of consciousness

Most of the actions we perform in everyday life, and even many of the experiences that affect our actions, *can* happen quite well on a sub-conscious level. Emotions can be subconscious—people may be said to be "not in touch with their feelings". Desires are quite often kept out of consciousness, especially if they are socially unacceptable ones. Over-learned actions require very little in the way of consciousness—we are capable of performing extremely complicated acts like typing our thoughts onto a computer or driving home from work without being at all

---

3 Population spikes are extracellular field potentials generated by the coordinated firing of action potentials in a group of cells.

conscious of the details of what we are doing. In an emergency we often make quite complex decisions and act on them very fast, on a completely sub-conscious basis—we "act first and think later". We sometimes even make more leisurely decisions about what to do in a novel situation by withdrawing the conscious mind and allowing the right answer to simply "come"—all the work involved in weighing up pros and cons, assigning weights to various factors according to current overall goals and figuring out the best solution is then done on a sub-conscious level and the decision simply presents itself as a *fait accompli* to the conscious mind. In fact creativity, which we feel to be one of the major features that distinguishes us humans in all our conscious glory from present-day computers, actually seems to operate best on an unconscious level. The "aha!" experience is a well-documented feature of the mental life of unusually creative persons. In this kind of creativity, the most effective strategy seems to be feed in all the relevant information, chew it over consciously for a bit and then forget about the problem. The creative solution then simply pops into mind some time later, when the subject is doing something completely different, or even sleeping. The point is, while consciousness *may* be involved to a greater or lesser extent in all these features of life, it does not seem to be actually *necessary* for any of them. So what, one might wonder, is the good of it?

In fact, consciousness seems actually to be *required* in only two circumstances: (1) when we are in the learning phase of acquiring new information or a new skill (which is generally accepted as requiring access to the hippocampus or cerebellum) and (2) to access the language system.

As we have seen in Chapter 1, while the concepts of consciousness and attention are theoretically distinct, consciousness is at the very least intimately associated attention. One can not be fully conscious of something without paying attention to it and conversely one can not pay attention to something without its entering consciousness (except possibly in the anomalous case of brain-damaged "blindsight" patients, where attention to a particular location in space apparently enhances detection of stimuli at that location in the absence of consciousness of these stimuli (Kentridge, Heywood, & Weiskrantz, 1999)). Similarly, learning is only readily accomplished if one pays attention to (and therefore is conscious of) the thing that is to be learned [4, 5]. The biological importance of this requirement to pay attention when learning is obvious: if brains stored a representation of absolutely everything that happened to the organism and not just the important things to which attention was paid, the system would soon saturate.

So in almost all circumstances, consciousness appears to be necessary (though unfortunately, as any harassed student in exam week will tell you, not sufficient) for learning. In this context it is interesting that the major structures in the brain that are known to be involved in learning are the hippocampus and the cerebellum (see Chapter 1). As shown in the earlier sections of this chapter, the hippocampus and the cerebellum are exactly the places where the importance of electric field effects in normal function has been demonstrated. It is not currently known exactly how the hippocampus operates in processing sensory information so that it can be stored in long-term memory, but what can be said is that (a) consciousness is necessary for learning and thus arguably for accessing the hippocampus (b) spatiotemporal patterns in the electromagnetic field are somehow involved in normal hippocampal function (c) the hypothesis put forward in this book is that spatiotemporal patterns in the electromagnetic field are identical with consciousness. Clearly this is an area of some interest, which would repay further experimental study.

---

4   There is some evidence for subliminal learning of single words but the information capacity of this system is very limited.
5   So-called implicit learning (where the subject is supposed to have no awareness of what is being learned) is a controversial topic, but all agree that minimally one must pay attention to and therefore be conscious of the actual subject matter, although one may not be able to articulate the underlying rules and regularities about the subject matter that are learned.

CHAPTER EIGHT: OBJECTIONS TO THE THEORY

❖ *Lack of effect of environmental fields on consciousness*
❖ *Lack of evidence for telepathy*
❖ *Split consciousness with split brains*
❖ *Theory same as Kohler's and already disproved by Lashley*
❖ *Lack of evidence that fields process information*
❖ *Lack of advantages of this theory over the Neural Identity Theory*

Like any theory worth its salt, the one being put forward here has been the subject of a number of challenges, most of which are listed below. I would like to emphasize that none of these objections is a straw man. All have actually been put forward in opposition to the theory—most of them by anonymous journal referees, but some by friends or by people who at least were willing to sign their names to their misgivings. These objections are as follows:

(1) If consciousness is a pattern in the electromagnetic field, one would expect that electric fields like those generated by power cables or domestic mains voltages, or magnetic fields such as those generated by MRI (magnetic resonance imaging) machines should directly affect consciousness. They demonstrably do not. Therefore the theory must be wrong.

(2) If consciousness is an oscillation in the electromagnetic field then it should be able to be radiated by the brain and therefore telepathy should at the very least be more common than it is (assuming that one believes it ever does occur). Telepathy is actually rare or non-existent—certainly not an everyday phenomenon. Therefore the theory must be wrong.

126

(3) If, as proposed, the consciousness of an individual is the totality of the conscious configurations of the electromagnetic field that is associated with that individual's brain, then cutting the corpus callosum should have no noticeable effects on consciousness, since the field generated by one half of the brain is still contiguous with the field generated by the other half. But this operation apparently produces two individual consciousnesses associated with the one brain. Therefore the theory must be wrong.

(4) This is not a new theory—it was the secret hope of early EEG workers and it was put forward by Popper. However it was tested and disproved by Kohler, Lashley and Sperry in the 1940s and 50s. The theory has already been shown to be wrong.

(5) You haven't shown that electromagnetic fields can actually process information, as consciousness can. Neurons can do information processing, either by acting as switches or by acting as analogue systems, but there is no evidence that electromagnetic fields can perform that kind of computing. But consciousness does do information processing. Therefore the theory can't be accepted.

(6) This theory has no obvious advantages over the Neural Identity theory (which basically says that the firing of neurons *per se* is identical with consciousness). Therefore the theory shouldn't be accepted.

Answers to the objections

Objection 1: If consciousness is a pattern in the electromagnetic field, one would expect that electric fields like those generated by power cables or domestic mains voltages, or magnetic fields such as those generated by MRI (magnetic resonance imaging) machines should directly affect consciousness. They demonstrably do not. Therefore the theory must be wrong.

Answer to Objection 1

It is certainly true that no subjectively discernable changes in consciousness are produced by the proximity of a wall socket or an overhead power transmission line. However it is not true that such changes would be expected. The rate of radiation of energy by oscillations of any field is proportional to the fourth power of the frequency of the oscillations, so at mains voltages of 230 or 110 volts the amount of radiation generated by oscillations at 50 or 60 Hz is tiny. While mains voltage can certainly introduce artefacts into the recording of EEGs, by inducing currents in the wires connecting the recording electrodes to the amplifiers, it simply does not produce strong enough radiation to alter the intricate spatial electromagnetic configurations proposed to be consciousness at their generation sites in the brain. If major external electric currents are passed directly through the brain, as in electroconvulsive therapy, there are genuine disruptions of the electric fields within the brain and there are also major disruptions in consciousness. (This can only be regarded as supportive and not conclusive evidence for the present hypothesis however, since electroconvulsive therapy also changes patterns of neural firing and various other physiological parameters). But it is highly unlikely that radiation from domestic power lines could induce any disruption of the electric field patterns in the brain.

On the other hand, the magnets in MRI machines do produce huge magnetic fields, which should in principle be large enough to affect intracerebral electromagnetic configurations. It is also true that the only changes in consciousness that are occasionally experienced in MRI machines are some visual scintillations, which are generally thought to be caused by firing of neurons induced by the machine-generated electromagnetic fluctuations. As with radiated 50 Hz electric fields, the external magnetic fields generated by an MRI machine certainly do affect the recording of EEG waveforms, by inducing currents in the recording hardware, but the question still is whether there could be any effective coupling between the imposed magnetic fields and the kinds of intricate spatial electromagnetic configurations proposed as being consciousness. In other words, do the magnetic fields in an MRI machine materially affect the brain-generated spatiotemporal configurations we are talking about at their source?

This is a question probably best attacked empirically. Recent advances in technology have allowed the recording of EEGs inside MRI machines and the answer seems to be that once the recording artefacts are dealt with, the magnetic field in MRI machines does not significantly affect the EEG (Allen, Polizzi, Krakow, Fish, & Lemieux, 1998; Jenkins, et al., 1996; Muri, et al., 1998). Of course more such studies will be necessary when the precise spatiotemporal patterns that covary with particular sensory experiences have been identified. In fact this is a very good potential source of disconfirming data, but the indications so far are good for the theory.

Objection 2: If consciousness is an oscillation in the electromagnetic field then it should be able to be radiated by the brain and therefore telepathy should at the very least be more common than it is (assuming that one believes it ever does occur). Telepathy is actually rare or non-existent—certainly not an everyday phenomenon. Therefore the theory must be wrong.

Answer to Objection 2

The answer to Objection 2 is closely related to the answer to Objection 1. It concerns the known physics of electromagnetic radiation. The frequency of the major electromagnetic oscillations generated by the brain is in the range from 1 to about 100 Hz, with most of the power below around 45 Hz. The wavelength of 40 Hz electromagnetic oscillations can be calculated (by dividing the speed of light by the frequency of the oscillations) at approximately 8,000 km. The optimal length of antenna for picking up a radio signal is about one wavelength, so the optimal length of antenna for picking up 40 Hz radiation would be 8,000 km (which is somewhat larger than the size of a human brain). As mentioned above, the rate of radiation of energy by oscillations of any field is proportional to the fourth power of the frequency of the oscillations. Therefore the energy radiated at 40 Hz by a power source like the brain would be so small that either an extremely sensitive detector or an antenna approximately 8,000 km long would be needed, even to detect a generalised broadcast signal. To retrieve any specific information, the signal would probably need to be carried by oscillations with a wavelength similar to the size of the brain, which translates to microwave frequencies. Thus on the present hypothesis telepathy would not, in fact, be expected to be a common event.

Interestingly however, there is some evidence that external modulation of the brain's electromagnetic field can modulate conscious experience. For example:

(a) Input to the brain of a very weak microwave carrier signal, amplitude modulated at EEG frequencies, disrupts cognitive processes at energy levels that do not exhibit thermal effects and would not be expected to cause neural firing (Adey, 1977; Adey, 1979; Adey, 1981).

(b) Rats can learn to detect a 60 Hz vertical electric field, with a standard shape of psychometric function or stimulus-strength/detection curve (Sagan, Stell, Bryan, & Adey, 1987).

These findings both support the present hypothesis and leave open the possibility that if the present hypothesis is correct, telepathy might be expected occasionally to occur. This is not the place to attempt a critical review of the extensive scientific literature on telepathy, but it is interesting in an anecdotal way to note that an experience of telepathic communication with his sister in a moment of crisis is reported to have been the impetus that led Hans Berger to initiate his original work on the human EEG. It is also interesting that the speculations above suggest the idea that the signals we are looking for in brain-generated electromagnetic activity might actually not be in the ELF (extremely low frequency) range where everyone is presently looking, but could turn out to be closer to the microwave frequency range—which is of course always filtered out in present-day electrophysiological recordings.

Objection 3: *If, as proposed, the consciousness of an individual is the totality of the conscious configurations of the electromagnetic field that is associated with that individual's brain, then cutting the corpus callosum should have no noticeable effects on consciousness, since the field generated by one half of the brain is still contiguous with the field generated by the other half. But this operation apparently produces two individual consciousnesses associated with the one brain. Therefore the theory must be wrong.*

Answer to Objection 3

This objection goes to a theory that purports to explain self consciousness, which the present theory does not. As pointed out in Chapter 1, the present theory is, at least at this stage, confined to simple consciousness. However the objection is a cogent one and deserves to be addressed.

Again, empirical findings must take precedence over predictions. A little delving into the voluminous empirical literature on split brains quickly reveals that, far from having a "split personality", split brain patients are actually remarkable mainly for the fact that it is very difficult to detect any changes at all in their consciousness. In fact early investigators were led to the exasperated and facetious conclusion that the purpose of the corpus callosum "must be mainly mechanical…to keep the hemispheres from sagging" (Lashley quoted by Kandel et al (Kandel, Schwartz, & Jessell, 1995). It was not until Roger Sperry performed a series of clever experiments involving presentation of sensory input to only one half of the brain (a situation which virtually never occurs in everyday life) that the separation of right brain from left brain in commissurotomised patients could be detected behaviorally at all (Sperry, 1982; Sperry, 1984; Sperry, 1966; Sperry, 1968). Recent work in what then became a huge research field arrives at the conclusion that, in the case of vision for example, interhemispheric transfer of information is not entirely absent in commissurotomised subjects. There appear to be two systems, one of which can be split and the other which can not (Corballis, 1994; Corballis, 1995). There is no universally accepted explanation for the fact that part of the system of visual experience can not be split by cutting the corpus callosum. One possibility is that this system is subserved by the conscious field.

Objection 4: This is not a new theory—it was the secret hope of early EEG workers and it was put forward by Popper. However it was tested and disproved by Kohler, Lashley and Sperry in the 1940s and 50s. The theory has already been shown to be wrong.

Answer to Objection 4

As mentioned above, it is quite likely that Hans Berger did secretly hope to discover the secrets of consciousness by studying the EEG. However, being a good Teutonic scientist, he was careful never to state this in print—and none of the other early EEG workers made any such statements either, at least to my knowledge. The present theory was certainly not put forward in Karl Popper's published writings. Again to my knowledge, even Wolfgang Kohler never actually proposed in so many words that consciousness was identical with certain configurations in the electromagnetic field, although his Field Theory certainly skirts around the issue. The experiments by Lashley and Sperry which are often misconstrued as being adequate tests of either Kohler's theory or the present one are discussed in Chapter 7. In my view they do not disprove either hypothesis.

Objection 5: You haven't shown that electromagnetic fields can actually process information, as consciousness can. Neurons can do information processing, either by acting as switches or by acting as analogue systems, but there is no evidence that electromagnetic fields can perform that kind of computing. But consciousness does do information processing. Therefore the theory can't be accepted at this stage.

Answer to Objection 5

This objection can be approached from two angles:

(a) by asking whether consciousness actually does do information processing

(b) by asking whether electromagnetic fields can do information processing

(a) Cognitive psychologists think in terms of information processing. Therefore, to a cognitive scientist, the only kind of theory of consciousness which is acceptable is a functional theory, which deals with information processing. However, prolonged thought about question (a) above (involving both conscious and unconscious manipulation of the problem) suggests that the only available answer to the question of whether consciousness itself can do information processing may be "no". To throw it back on our objector, we could ask that he first demonstrate unequivocally that consciousness DOES perform information processing. It is remarkably difficult to come up with even a single example of a situation where information processing can actually be shown to be done by consciousness itself, rather than by the unconscious brain processes that underlie it. Almost certainly all the processing required to produce sensory gestalts is unconscious. Generalised answers such as the blanket statement that consciousness must be good for something because otherwise it would not have been selected by evolution, or that consciousness is "supremely functional—we can not do much without it" really do not cut the mustard—we need a concrete EXAMPLE of a situation in which consciousness *per se* actually does something useful that could not be explained as being done by a non-conscious neural process. If our objector can not produce this, then there is basically no objection to be answered. If consciousness can not be shown to perform information processing over and above that which is performed unconsciously, then we need not show how electromagnetic fields perform information processing.

This is not entirely a comfortable response to the objection as stated however. The reader fresh from Chapter 7 may notice a certain ambivalence here about whether consciousness *per se* does or does not have any causal effects (which could perhaps be equated with information processing, although it is not entirely clear just what the latter necessarily entails). Therefore it comes as some relief to note that

(b) electromagnetic fields almost certainly CAN perform a limited amount of information processing anyway, whether they are required to by this theory or not. The electromagnetic field is a vector quantity and the principle of superposition applies to it (Halliday, Resnick, & Walker, 1993). This principle says that when several effects occur simultaneously, their net effect is the sum of individual effects. In other words, configurations of the electromagnetic field sum algebraically. Therefore, a kind of math can indeed be considered to be performed when one spatiotemporal electromagnetic pattern encounters another such pattern. The outcome of this math then can (as shown in Chapter 7) be translated into a spatiotemporal effect on the pattern of firing of neurons.

The information processing possible using this kind of volume conduction mechanism is almost certainly blunter (less accurate and in some ways slower) than that possible using the precise digital properties of neuron-to-neuron transmission—but then so is the information processing that is postulated to occur in the conscious "global workspace" which is proposed by the leading process theory of consciousness (Baars, 1988).

Objection 6: This theory has no obvious advantages over the Neural Identity theory (which basically says that brain events per se are identical with consciousness). Therefore the theory can't be accepted at this stage.

Answer to Objection 6

This objection is basically a statement that the psychoneural identity theory currently has possession of the minds of nine tenths of the biologists who think about these matters and that possession is nine tenths of the law. Against this it can be argued that even if the electromagnetic field theory did have no advantages over the neural identity theory, it is not necessarily the case that whatever theory appeared on the scene first is necessarily the right one.

However, it is true that most biologists at the end of the twentieth century do uncritically accept the psychoneural identity theory and therefore feel that even the consideration of any other theory is an unnecessary waste of time. So a discussion of the shortcomings of the psychoneural identity theory and a comparison of these with the advantages of the electromagnetic field theory is probably inevitable.

The first problem we encounter in attempting to discuss the psychoneural identity theory, however, is the lack of a clear statement of that theory. The generally accepted meaning of psychoneural identity is that consciousness is identical with brain events. But with what feature of brain events is it proposed that consciousness is identical? Obviously it is not simply the physical anatomy of the brain which is identical with consciousness, because in that case the brains of newly dead persons (or sleeping or anesthetised persons) would still be conscious. Perhaps it is the case that neural tissue contains some undiscovered Factor X—a chemical perhaps—which bestows the property of consciousness and disappears on death (or during sleep or anesthesia). In that case only some sorts of neural tissue must carry this factor and then only intermittently, because most of what goes on in the brain is not conscious for most of the time. This latter fact also poses a problem for the idea that the firing of action potentials *per se* is identical with consciousness. The peripheral motor nerves in the big toe fire action potentials and these are (almost) identical with the action potentials in the visual cortex, in terms of the movement of ions through membrane channels that underlies them. Is the big toe conscious? Most neurobiologists would say that it is not. But is the visual cortex conscious? Probably. Sometimes. So what's the difference? Well, if action potentials themselves are uniform in kind, perhaps there are "awareness neurons" which have special ways of firing action potentials. Perhaps particular kinds of bursts of action potential firing constitute consciousness, for example. This doesn't seem very likely and there is no evidence whatsoever connecting the idea to the realities of consciousness as measured in the laboratory. We're definitely struggling here.

Finally, we are forced to the conclusion that the only viable formulation of the psychoneural identity theory is that of the emergent-property theorist. Roger Sperry (Sperry, 1969) argues that consciousness is an emergent property of matter organized as nervous tissue. By this he means that consciousness is something "different from and more than" the sum of its parts, which emerges out of the complex spatiotemporal interaction of billions of neural elements. One more step and this would be the electromagnetic field theory of consciousness. But Sperry did not take that step.

So the ultimate version of the psychoneural identity theory turns out to be a close cousin—a precursor perhaps—of the electromagnetic field theory. Let us examine the advantages of taking the final step, from a version of the psychoneural identity theory which proposes that consciousness is identical with the spatiotemporally patterned firing of large masses of neurons, to the electromagnetic field theory which proposes that consciousness is identical with the patterns in the electromagnetic field produced by the firing of those neurons.

First, there is the issue of whether the firing of neurons *per se* can even be regarded as a member of the same category of phenomena as the subjective experience of the color blue. It simply does not seem to make intuitive or even logical sense to postulate identity between the subjective experience of blueness and the movement of ions into and out of cells in area V4 of the cerebral cortex. What does it mean to say that two entities are identical?

Following Leibnitz's law as to the strict identity of indiscernables, to say that consciousness is identical with neural events is to say that these two possess all of their properties in common. But it seems patently obvious that the subjective experience of the color blue and the firing of action potentials in V4 have strikingly different properties, rather than all properties in common. On the other hand it seems more possible that the subjective experience of blueness should have all properties in common with a particular configuration of the electromagnetic field. Other configurations of the electromagnetic field apparently do have a wide variety of wonderful properties, so it seems not unreasonable that some configurations of the field should have the wonderful property of consciousness. In short, it simply seems less unlikely that a person should be identified with an everchanging, shimmering, invisible field that is spatially coincident with their brain than that they should be "nothing but a pack of neurons."

Secondly, the psychoneural identity theory implies that only neural tissue—and only certain kinds of neural tissue at that—can embody consciousness. In some sense this postulate necessarily involves "smuggling dualism in through the back door" as Globus puts it (Globus, 1973). What is it about matter that is organized as neural tissue that makes it potentially identical with consciousness, while matter organized in other ways is not? The psychoneural identity theory offers no clues. The electromagnetic field theory is not subject to this difficulty, however, as it admits the possibility that any kind of matter capable of generating the relevant configurations of the field could support consciousness.

Summary

None of the objections so far advanced against acceptance of the electromagnetic field theory of consciousness has much real force and certainly none of them even comes close to being fatal to the theory.

CHAPTER NINE: GOD, DARWIN AND THE ELECTROMAGNETIC FIELD THEORY OF CONSCIOUSNESS

Most people who have lived in the period from the evolution of *Homo sapiens* to the end of the 20th century—and indeed probably most of those presently alive—have believed or do believe that there is more to the universe than can be apprehended by the senses and more to the nature of persons than the body. I can put these ideas no more poetically than did the late Dean of St Paul's William Sherlock, who wrote in 1751 (Sherlock, 1751)

> "...for when we die, we do not fall into nothing, or into a profound fleep, into a ftate of filence and infenfibility till the refurrection; but we only change our place, and our dwelling, we remove out of this world, and leave our bodies to fleep in the earth till the refurrection, but our fouls and fpirits ftill live in an invifible ftate. I fhall not go about to prove thefe things, but take it for granted that you all believe them; for that we leave this world, and that our bodies rot and putrify in the grave, needs no proof, for we can fee it with our eyes; and that our fouls cannot die, but are by nature immortal, has been the belief of all mankind."

A century or so later, Charles Darwin threw an almighty spanner into the works of this universally accepted idea (Darwin, 1859). The concept that life evolved by natural selection turned all varieties of religion on their heads at a stroke. It simply removed any need for a designing God to create all the various and multitudinous manifestations of life. According to the theory of evolution it was all done, if not quite with mirrors, then at least with similarly mechanical algorithms of stunning simplicity. Evolution is a mindless process. In its scheme of things, Mind did not come first, as it so clearly had in the ontologies of the various great religions that had held sway in previous millennia. Instead of one great Mind which created and controlled everything, this upstart new theory had it that a multitude of smaller minds simply evolved, over the course of many slow eons, from nothingness. It is difficult to overestimate the magnitude of the conceptual shift this new way of looking at things required.

To philosophical giants like Berkeley and Hume, everything was a manifestation of Mind. The universe was essentially God's dream. To the molecular biologist of today, this view is so entirely foreign as to be ludicrous—a historical curiosity, if it is known at all. In fact, as a direct result of the success of the theory of evolution, most biologists for the last century or so have, at least publically, rejected the ideas of an immortal soul, an afterlife, or a personal God. It must be said that such a rejection is still statistically abnormal in the broader population and indeed privately these ideas have probably been more tenacious even among scientists than many have chosen to admit; but to the world at least, biological science nowadays presents a uniform face of stout and stoical atheism. What Dennett memorably calls Darwin's dangerous idea (Dennett, 1995) had the major effect of splitting religion and science wide apart.

The idea central to the present book may not be as great or as dangerous as Darwin's, but it does have modest implications in the same territory. In one sense, the present theory can be seen as knitting up the ravell'd sleeve of spirituality and undoing the schism between science and religion that was caused by the raw effects of the theory of evolution. It does so in the following very straightforward way.

If simple consciousness is indeed identical with certain localized configurations of the electromagnetic field, then the electromagnetic field as a whole (which as far as we know pervades the entire universe) includes all of the conscious configurations that currently exist in the universe. The electromagnetic field as a whole can thus be thought of as one vast mind.

This concept relies on the understanding that the electromagnetic phenomena that are produced by simple material objects such as magnets (or more complicated ones such as brains) are not isolated individual fields generated *de novo* by the objects, as basic physics texts tend to suggest, but localized perturbations in a universal, all-pervading field which is presently known as The Electromagnetic Field. The present theory is that simple consciousness is identical with certain localized patterns of perturbation in this field, which are produced by the action of brains. So according to the present theory, The Electromagnetic Field contains an array of localized spots of consciousness that are spatially coincident with an array of brains, with quite large areas of non-consciousness between the spots of consciousness. When these spots of conscious experience are coincident with a human (or probably any higher primate) brain, they are integrated into a similarly localized system which feels itself to be the individual experiencer of all the conscious experiences generated by (or perhaps simply in close proximity to) that particular brain. However, when the spots of conscious experience are coincident with a non-human brain or an undeveloped human brain, this is not necessarily the case. Then simple conscious experiences almost certainly still exist, but there is probably no self-consciousness associated with them. In the hypothetical situation of the spots of conscious experience's being generated by hardware rather than wetware, there would almost certainly not be any self-consciousness associated with the simple consciousness—in fact according to the present theory, it should be possible to generate a little isolated blob of middle-C-experience in one corner of the room. If you have difficulty thinking of an isolated blob of conscious experience without an experiencer, then you might like to consider The Electromagnetic Field as a whole as the overall experiencer of all of the conscious experiences that are currently happening in the universe. And another name for the overall experiencer of all the conscious experiences in the universe would be a universal mind.

Whether or not this universal mind itself has a Self and whether It is capable of initiating any actions are further questions, into which we will not delve at this stage. The point is that if the idea presented in this book is true, then the universe as a whole is conscious. Furthermore, this universal consciousness can be thought of as continuously experiencing, in real time, every sensation and perception, every thought, every emotion that is generated by the mind of every conscious being in the universe.

If this is not a description of what humans through the ages have conceived of as God, then it must come pretty close.

The electromagnetic field theory of consciousness and mystical experience

Seen in this context, the core "mystical" experience which, at least according to Bucke's great late-nineteenth century classic (Bucke, 1993) happened to all of the founders of the world's great religions and was the immediate cause of their becoming spiritual leaders, straight away becomes to some extent understandable. This so-called mystical experience is widely reported as being ineffable, but it can be considered no less real for that—after all the experience of the color red is similarly indescribable if one is speaking to someone blind from birth. Insofar as it can be described in words, the experience in question involves a direct, unassailably real appreciation of the fact that "all is one".For this reason it is often called the unity experience. The continuous state of consciousness into which the unity experience sometimes pitches its subjects is called by Bucke cosmic consciousness.

Now, while there is no denying the reality of the unity experience to those who have it, there are two possibilities as to how it may be understood. It could simply be an unusual sensation, which is generated internally by the brain of the experiencer and bears the same relation to the outside world as does a dream. Alternatively, the unity experience may represent an accurate perception of some reality that exists outside the brain of the subject. At present we have no way of distinguishing between these two alternatives. However, the theory put forward here at least provides some framework on which to hang the idea that the second alternative might be the correct one. If the all-pervading electromagnetic field is in fact conscious, then the unity experience simply represents the sudden realization by one tiny conscious fragment of the field that it is not, after all, isolated and alone in its immediate surround of bone and flesh, but is in fact an inalienable part of the vast, glorious whole.

Relationship of the electromagnetic field theory of consciousness to the theory of evolution

At this stage I would like to emphasize that while the present theory can be seen as undoing some of the deleterious effects that were produced by the rather hysterical initial response to Darwinism, it in no way refutes or requires rejection of Mr Darwin's great theory. The present theory is quite compatible with the view that consciousness was not present in the universe before its biological evolution.

If we take this view, then humans were not created by God so much as the other way around. We (collectively) *are* God. The overall universal consciousness (which can be named God, Allah, Brahman, Gaia, Yahweh, or whatever you like) would simply have evolved as our own human consciousness evolved. The more conscious individuals appear in the world, the more complex God becomes. Such a viewpoint accords humankind both great power and great responsibility.

On the other hand, the present theory is also compatible with the notion that consciousness did exist in the universe before it evolved biologically. Take your pick.

APPENDIX A

The Psychophysical Laws

As a result of a huge amount of experimental work over the last 150 or more years, there have been delineated a few relationships between physical stimuli in the world outside the human nervous system and subjective sensory experience of these stimuli which have achieved the status of "laws". These psychophysical laws have a rather different standing from purely physical laws (which describe physical phenomena such as the falling of apples and the movement of planets) because the psychological phenomena on which psychophysical laws are based are much less precise and harder to measure than physical phenomena. Nevertheless, such psychophysical laws as are currently accepted should probably be included in the facts that would have to be explained by a theory of consciousness. The most basic of the so-called psychophysical laws are stated as follows.

Weber's Law

If X and $X + DX$ are the magnitudes of two stimuli that can just be distinguished from each other (i.e. that are "just noticeably different"), then Weber's Law says that

$$\Delta X / X = \Theta$$

where Θ is a constant for each sensory attribute.

In words, *the bigger a sensory stimulus, the bigger has to be the change in that stimulus before any difference can be noticed subjectively.*

This empirical generalization was first stated by Weber in 1834, to describe both his own data on the discrimination of weights hefted simultaneously by both hands and on the visual discrimination of the length of lines, and the findings of others on auditory discrimination of the frequency of tones. It was named Weber's Law by Fechner in 1860, though Fechner noted that in some cases, the data available by that time were actually better fit by the equation

$$\Delta X/(X+X_0) = \Theta$$

where X_0 is a small constant.

In the auditory system, for example, a large number of empirical studies have established that Weber's Law holds accurately for the discrimination of the level of Gaussian noise, but not for the amplitude of a pure tone (Laming, 1986).

Fechner's Logarithmic Law

From Weber's Law and certain additional assumptions—for example the assumption that sensation differences corresponding to just noticeable differences in sensation (sensation jnd's) are equal, Fechner deduced his famous logarithmic law:

$$\Psi = k \log \Phi$$

where Ψ is a sensation and Φ is its stimulus. To state this law in words, *a sensation is proportional to the logarithm of its stimulus.* Fechner's law immediately became the subject of enormous controversy and was eventually excoriated by none other than that paragon of psychological virtue William James. However to this day it still forms the basis of the universally used decibel scale of loudness, which relates perceived loudness in decibels (dB) to the logarithm of the ratio between the measured sound intensity, I and a reference sound intensity, I_{ref} :

$$dB = 10 \log (I/I_{ref})$$

The use of the decibel scale reflects the fact that, roughly speaking, *a sound only doubles in perceived loudness when the physical intensity of the sound increases ten-fold.* [6] This means that the auditory system of humans

---

6 Since sound intensity is proportional to sound pressure squared, this equation can
   also be written as
dB = 10 log $(p/p_{ref})^2$ = 20 log (p/p_{ref}) where p is sound pressure. This formulation allows direct relation of sensation to the physical properties of the stimulus.

can deal with a huge range of sound intensity without being over-whelmed. It also places a very useful empirical constraint on any hypo-thesis concerning the electromagnetic pattern which constitutes the sensation of a sound.

Stevens' Power Law

While Fechner measured sensation by means of the just noticeable dif-ference or jnd, S.S. Stevens employed units defined by ratio and interval scales[7] and concluded that The Psychophysical Law is not a logarithmic law but a power law (e.g. (Stevens, 1957)). Stevens suggested that, for example, loudness L, is a power function of the physical intensity of the sound I, such that

$$L = k \, I^{0.3}$$

where k is a constant that depends on the subject and the units used. In other words, *the perceived loudness of a given sound is proportional to its physical intensity raised to the power of 0.3.*

To generalize, this equation can be written as:

$$\Psi = \Phi^n$$

where Ψ is the magnitude of a sensation in psychological units, Φ is the magnitude of the stimulus in physical units and n is an exponent that varies in magnitude with the dimension being scaled—e.g. n is 0.3 for loudness, 0.3—0.5 for intensity of light, 1.0 for taste and so on.

Stevens' work led to the rise of what some have called "the new psychophysics" (Gescheider, 1997) and dozens of investigators have

---

7 A ratio scale asks the subject to assign numerals to a series of stimuli to represent their felt ratios. In other words, the subject should assign weight 4 to Φ_2 and weight 2 to Φ_1 only if Φ_2 feels twice as heavy as Φ_1. An interval scale asks the subject to assign numerals to a series of stimuli to represent their felt equality of intervals e.g. the subject is to assign weight 3 to Φ_1, weight 4 to Φ_2 and weight 5 to Φ_3 only if Φ_3 feels as much heavier than Φ_2 as Φ_2 feels heavier than Φ_1.

confirmed his power law. However, it will be apparent that none of these so-called psychophysical laws measures the quantity of sensation in absolute terms. All measurements of sensation are couched in terms of the relationship of the sensation of interest to other sensations evoked by other stimuli. In fact the results obtained tend to depend on the measurement method used and on the environmental conditions when the measurements are made. There are many exceptions to the power law (Gescheider, 1997).

In summary, psychophysics is a huge and complicated field of study. For our present purposes, it is perhaps sufficient to state that (a) the measurement of subjective sensations is fraught with difficulty and (b) it is relatively rare for the magnitude of a measured sensation to covary on a one to one basis with the magnitude of its physical stimulus.

APPENDIX B

A Beginner's Guide to Cellular Neurophysiology

The Resting Membrane Potential

The central fact of cellular neurophysiology is that the inside of nerve cells is slightly electrically negative with respect to the outside. This situation arises because the chemical composition of the intracellular environment is different from the chemical composition of the extracellular environment. Relatively speaking, there is a high concentration potassium ions inside the cell and a low concentration outside. Since the membrane separating the inside contents of the cell from the outside fluid is somewhat permeable to potassium ions under normal conditions, these ions tend to diffuse out of the cell (simply because there is a natural tendency for any particle in a watery environment to diffuse from areas where there is a lot of it to areas where there isn't). As positively charged potassium ions leave the cell, the intracellular environment becomes more and more electrically negative. Opposite charges attract, so eventually this intracellular negativity becomes strong enough to prevent any more potassium ions leaving the cell. The force of the concentration gradient influencing the ions to leave the cell is now equalled by the opposing force of the electrical gradient influencing them to go back in. The intracellular voltage at which this situation obtains is called the *equilibrium potential* for potassium and is about -90 mv.

Most neurons sit for most of the time at an intracellular *resting membrane potential* that is slightly less negative than the equilibrium potential for potassium. However there are various ways in which the resting membrane potential of neurons can suddenly be changed.

Action potentials

Firstly, the neuron can fire an action potential. Action potentials involve sodium ions. The concentration situation for sodium ions (which also carry one positive charge) is the opposite of that for potassium ions i.e. there is a lot more sodium outside the cell than inside. Most of the time the cell membrane is completely impermeable to sodium ions, but there do exist sodium channels (i.e. protein-lined pores in the lipid membrane which can open to let sodium ions flow through them) which are voltage dependent. When the inside of the cell for one reason or another becomes less negative, these voltage dependent channels suddenly open and sodium rushes into the cell. Because the concentration gradient for sodium is opposite to that for potassium, the equilibrium potential for sodium is +58 mV (as opposed to -90 mV for potassium). So if the sodium channels stayed open for long enough, the influx of sodium would continue until the inside of the cell was +58 mV with respect to the outside. Before that happens however, the changing internal voltage closes the sodium channels and opens a separate set of potassium channels. Whenever membrane channels open, ions flow through them in such a direction as to bring the intracellular potential towards the equilibrium potential for the ion involved, so potassium ions now flow out of the cell again until the resting membrane potential is restored.

This whole sequence of events takes only a few milliseconds. Thus an action potential consists of a sharp spike of intracellular positivity. Because of the characteristics of the sodium channels involved, action potentials are "all-or-none" events. Once the threshold membrane voltage is reached (about -45 mV) they either happen or don't happen, with no shades of gray. As such, action potentials provide neurons with what is essentially a digital coding capability; on or off, yes or no, 0 or 1.

Action potentials have two more important characteristics. They propagate down axons (a) very fast and (b) non-decrementally. Thus they are well adapted for conveying information over large distances in a remark-ably reliable fashion.

Excitatory and inhibitory postsynaptic potentials (epsps and ipsps)

The other main way in which the resting membrane potential of neurons can be altered is by means of postsynaptic potentials. These can be either excitatory (i.e. tending to bring the neuron towards the threshold for firing an action potential) or inhibitory (i.e. tending to keep the neuron away from the threshold for firing an action potential).

The gap between neurons where information passes from one to the other is called a synapse. Synapses usually involve the axon of one neuron (which is called the presynaptic neuron when speaking of this particular synapse) making a contact on one of the dendrites of another neuron, (which is called the postsynaptic neuron). When the action potential in the presynaptic axon reaches the axon terminal, it causes the release of vesicles of chemical neurotransmitter into the gap, or synaptic cleft. The neurotransmitter diffuses across the gap and interacts with transmitter receptors in the membrane of the postsynaptic cell. There are a number of different neurotransmitters in different kinds of neurons (one transmitter per neuron) and each kind of neurotransmitter has its own kinds of receptors, which are coupled to specific ion channels in the membrane of the postsynaptic cell. Interaction of a transmitter with its receptor opens (or occasionally closes) the ion channel associated with the receptor and ions then flow through the channel in such a way as to bring the internal voltage of the postsynaptic cell towards the equilibrium potential for the ion in question. The voltage changes brought about by these ion flows are called postsynaptic potentials.

Postsynaptic potentials differ from action potentials in one very impor-tant way. Postsynaptic potentials are not all-or-none events like action potentials—they are graded. This means that if more neurotransmitter has been released (as a result of more action potentials reaching the presynap-tic terminal) the postsynaptic potential will be bigger and longer-lasting.

If some of the postsynaptic receptors have been blocked by a drug, the postsynaptic potential will be smaller and shorter-lasting. If two postsynaptic potentials are evoked close together, in either time or space, they summate or add together to have a greater effect on the postsynaptic cell. This latter feature is very important, since it is rare that one epsp alone can bring a postsynaptic cell to the action potential threshold or one ipsp prevent firing. So while action potentials are essentially digital events, postsynaptic potentials are analogue ones. This becomes important in the generation of extracellular field potentials, which can be measured by EEG recordings.

The genesis of extracellular field potentials is described in Appendix C.

APPENDIX C

Generation of Extracellular Field Potentials

When neurotransmitter released by the nerve terminal acts on its postsynaptic receptors, ion channels open and positive ions flow into the postsynaptic cell, as described in Appendix B. The removal of these positive ions from the extracellular fluid leaves a measurable negativity in the area around the synapse. Therefore while an excitatory postsynaptic potential is happening, an extracellular electrode positioned near the synapse measures a negative-going synaptic potential. At the same time, because of the influx of positive ions in the synaptic region of the postsynaptic cell, a flow of current out of the cell in the non-synaptic regions is set up. If an electrode is placed outside a region of the cell that is not near the synapse, it records this outward current. Therefore the same synaptic potential recorded in these extrasynaptic regions is positive-going.

This change in sign of extracellular field potentials depending on the location of the recording electrode in relation to the synapse contrasts with the situation with intracellular recording, (where the recording electrode is inserted into the cell) when the postsynaptic potential is positive-going as a result of the influx of positive ions no matter where in the cell it is recorded.

In order to understand more about the generation of field potentials, knowledge of one physical law is needed. This is Ohm's Law, which can be stated as

$$V = I \times R$$

where V is voltage, I is current and R is resistance.

Electrophysiological potentials are measured as the voltage drop across a particular resistance. With intracellular recording, the relevant resistance is that of the cell membrane. With extracellular recording it is the

151

resistance of the extracellular fluid, which is usually very low compared to the resistance of the cell membrane. According to Ohm's Law, a given flow of current will produce a larger voltage across a large resistance than it will across a small resistance. Therefore, any given flow of ionic current produces a much bigger intracellular potential (i.e. voltage) than it does an extracellular potential. In fact in order for extracellular potentials to reach appreciable size, the field epsps from a number of spatially lined up cells have to summate. This means that the synapses have to be active synchronously. A high local extracellular resistance is also important in generation of relatively large field potentials.

Field potentials and the EEG

The EEG as measured by electrodes on the scalp is the sum total of all the field potentials that are generated within some unknown distance of the recording electrode. Clearly, those field potentials generated closest to the recording site will have the biggest influence on the waveforms recorded. In fact it is generally thought that only field potentials generated in the cerebral cortex are close enough to the scalp to be recordable by EEG electrodes at all. The case for this has never really been proven however. Certainly the first 10 milliseconds-worth of the auditory evoked potential is believed to be generated in the brainstem; but it is true that the amplitude of these waveforms is very small in comparison to the general EEG (i.e. fractions of a microvolt compared to about 50 microvolts for the total EEG).

The major difficulty about the interpretation of EEG recordings is that sorting out the cellular correlates of electrical activity which can only be measured many cm away from its site of generation is no easy matter. Even determining the general area in which a particular waveform in an evoked potential is generated is not straightforward. Calculating the detailed spatiotemporal configuration of an electromagnetic pattern at its generation site from measurements taken some distance away from that site is formidably difficult. This is known in mathematical and engineering circles as the inverse problem. Progress on description of the electromagnetic patterns covarying with conscious experience awaits an acceptable solution of the inverse problem for electroencephalographic measurements.

REFERENCES

Abraham, W.C., & Bear, M.F. (1996). Metaplasticity: the plasticity of synaptic plasticity. *Trends in Neuroscience, 19*, 126–130.

Adey, W.R. (1977). The sensorium and the modulation of cerebral states: tonic environmental influences on limbic and related systems. *Annals of the New York Academy of Sciences, 290*, 396–420.

Adey, W.R. (1979). Neurophysiologic effects of radiofrequency and microwave radiation. *Bulletin of the New York Academy of Medicine, 55*(11), 1079–93.

Adey, W.R. (1981). Tissue interactions with nonionizing electromagnetic fields. *Physiological Reviews, 61*(2), 435–514.

Adler, G., & Adler, J. (1989). Influence of stimulus intensity on AEP components in the 80– to 200–millisecond range. *Audiology, 28* 316–324.

Adrian, E.G. (1950). Sensory discrimination, with some recent evidence from the olfactory organ. *British Medical Bulletin, 6*, 330–332.

Akshoomoff, N.A., Courchesne, E., & Townsend, J. (1997). Attention coordination and anticipatory control. *International Review of Neurobiology, 41*, 575–598.

Alho, K. (1995). Cerebral generators of mismatch negativity (MMN) and its magnetic counterpart (MMNm) elicited by sound changes. *Ear and Hearing, 16*, 38–51.

Alho, K., Paavilainen, P., Reinikainen, K., Sams, M., & Naatanen, R. (1986). Separability of different negative components of the event-related potential associated with auditory stimulus processing. *Psychophysiology, 23*(6), 613–23.

Alho, K., Sams, M., Paavilainen, P., & Naatanen, R. (1986). Small pitch separation and the selective-attention effect on the ERP. *Psychophysiology, 23*(2), 189–97.

Alkon, D.L. (1983). Learning in a marine snail. *Scientific American, 249*, 70–84.

Allen, G., Buxton, R.B., Wong, E.C., & Courchesne, E. (1997). Attentional modulation of the cerebellum independent of motor involvement. *Science, 275*, 1940–1943.

Allen, P.J., Polizzi, G., Krakow, K., Fish, D.R., & Lemieux, L. (1998). Identification of EEG events in the MR scanner: the problem of pulse artefact and a method for its subtraction. *Neuroimage, 8*, 229–239.

Andersen, P., & Andersson, S.A. (1968). *Physiological basis of the alpha rhythm*. New York: Appleton-Century-Crofts.

Antrobus, J.S. (1983). REM and NONREM sleep reports: comparison of word frequency by cognitive classes. *Psychophysiology, 20*, 562–568.

Baars, B.J. (1988). *A cognitive theory of consciousness.* (1st ed.). Cambridge, New York: Cambridge University Press.

Baars, B.J. (1997a). *In the theatre of consciousness: the workspace of the mind*. Oxford, New York: Oxford University Press.

Baars, B.J. (1997b). Some essential differences between consciousness and attention, perception and working memory. *Consciousness and Cognition, 6*, 363–371.

Baddeley, A. (1992). Working memory. *Science, 255*, 556–559.

Badgaiyan, R.D., & Posner, M.I. (1998). Mapping the cingulate cortex in response selection and monitoring. *Neuroimage, 7*, 255–260.

Banquet, J.P. (1973). Spectral analysis of the EEG in meditation. *Electroencephalography and Clinical Neurophysiology, 35,* 14151.

Barlow, J.S. (1986). Artifact processing (rejection and minimization) in EEG data processing. In F.H.L.d. Silva, W.S.c. Leeuwen, & A. Remond (Eds.), *Clinical applications of computer analysis of EEG and other neurophysiological signals.* (Vol. 2, pp. 15–55). Amsterdam, New York, Oxford: Elsevier.

Barrie, J.M., Freeman, W.J., & Lenhart, M.D. (1996). Spatiotemporal analysis of prepyriform, visual, auditory, and somesthetic surface EEGs in trained rabbits. *Journal of Neurophysiology, 76*(1), 520–39.

Beaumont, J.G., & Rugg, M.D. (1979). The specificity of intrahemispheric EEG alpha coherence asymmetry related to the psychological task. *Biological Psychology, 9,* 237–248.

Belin, P., McAdams, S., Smith, B., Savel, S., Thivard, L., Samson, S., & Samson, Y. (1998). The functional anatomy of sound intensity discrimination. *Journal of Neuroscience, 18,* 6388–6394.

Benedict, R.H., Lockwood, A.H., Shucard, J.L., Shucard, D.W., Wack, D., & Murphy, B.W. (1998). Functional neuroimaging of attention in the auditory modality. *Neuroreport, 9,* 121–126.

Berger, H. (1929). Uber das elektroenkephalogram des menschen. *Arch. Psychiatr. Nervenkr., 87,* 527–570.

Bliss, T.V.P., & Gardner-Medwin, A.R. (1973). Long-lasting potentiation of synaptic transmission in the dentate area of the unanaesthetised rabbit following stimulation of the perforant path. *Journal of Physiology (London), 232,* 357–374.

Bliss, T.V.P., & Lomo, T. (1973). Long-lasting potentiation of synaptic transmission in the dentate area of the anaesthetised rabbit following stimulation of the perforant path. *Journal of Physiology (London)*, *232*, 331–356.

Bogen, J.E. (1995a). On the neurophysiology of consciousness: I. An overview. *Consciousness and Cognition*, *4*, 52–62.

Bogen, J.E. (1995b). On the neurophysiology of consciousness: Part II Constraining the semantic problem. *Consciousness and Cognition*, *4*, 137–158.

Bogen, J.E. (1997). Some neurophysiologic aspects of consciousness. *Seminars in Neurology*, *17*, 95–103.

Brazier, M.A.B., & Casby, J.U. (1952). Crosscorrelation and autocorrelation studies of electroencephalographic potentials. *Electroencephalography and Clinical Neurophysiology*, *4*, 201–211.

Breitmeyer, B.G., & Ganz, L. (1976). Implications of sustained and transient channels for theories of visual pattern masking, saccadic suppression, and information processing. *Psychological Review*, *83*(1), 1–36.

Bressler, S.L. (1984). Spatial organization of EEGs from olfactory bulb and cortex. *Electroencephalography and Clinical Neurophysiology*, *57*, 270–276.

Bressler, S.L., & Freeman, W.J. (1980). Frequency analysis of olfactory system EEG in cat, rabbit, and rat. *Electroencephalography & Clinical Neurophysiology*, *50*(1–2), 19–24.

Broadbent, D.E. (1958). *Perception and communication*. London: Pergamon Press.

Broca, P. (1861). Sur le siege de la faculte du language articule. *Bull. Soc. Anat. de Paris*, *6*, 355–369.

Brock, L.G., Coombs, J.S., & Eccles, J.C. (1952). The recording of potentials from motoneurones with an intracellular electrode. *Journal of Physiology (London)*, *117*, 431–460.

Brown, R.J., & Norcia, A.M. (1997). A method for investigating binocular rivalry in real time with the steady state VEP. *Vision Research*, *37*, 2401–2408.

Bruneau, N., Roux, S., Guerin, P., Garreau, B., & Lelord, G. (1993). Auditory stimulus intentsity responses and frontal midline theta rhythm. *Electroencephalography and Clinical Neurophysiology*, *86*, 213–216.

Buchel, C., & Friston, K.J. (1997). Modulation of connectivity in visual pathways by attention: cortical interactions evaluated with structural equation modelling and fMRI. *Cerebral Cortex*, *7*, 768–778.

Buchel, C., Josephs, O., Rees, G., Turner, R., Frith, C.D., & Friston, K.J. (1998). The functional anatomy of attention to visual motion. A functional MRI study. *Brain*, *121*, 1281–1294.

Buck, B.H., Black, S.E., Behrmann, M., Caldwell, C., & Bronskill, M.J. (1997). Spatial and object-based attentional deficits in Alzheimer's disease. Relationship to HMPAO-SPECT measures of parietal perfusion. *Brain*, *120*, 1229–1244.

Bucke, R.M. (1993). *Cosmic consciousness: a study in the evolution of the human mind.* New York: Citadel Press.

Cajal, S.R. (1911). *Histologie du Systeme Nerveux de l'homme et des vertebres.* (Vol. 2) (Azoulay L. Madrid, Trans.): Institutio Ramon y Cajal 1952.

Carter, C.S., Mintun, M., & Cohen, J.D. (1995). Interference and facilitation effects during selective attention: an H215O PET study of Stroop task performance. *Neuroimage, 2,* 264–272.

Carter, C.S., Mintun, M., Nichols, T., & Cohen, J.D. (1997). Anterior cingulate gyrus dysfunction and selective attention deficits in schizophrenia: [15O]H2O PET study during single-trial Stroop task performance. *American Journal of Psychiatry, 154,* 1670–1675.

Castro, C.A., Silbert, L.H., McNaughton, B.L., & Barnes, C.A. (1989). Recovery of spatial learning deficits after decay of electrically induced synaptic enhancement in the hippocampus. *Nature, 342,* 545–548.

Cavallero, C., Cicogna, P., Natale, V., Occhionero, M., & Zito, A. (1992). Slow wave sleep dreaming. *Sleep, 15,* 562–566.

Cavallero, C., Foulkes, D., Hollifield, M., & Terry, R. (1990). Memory sources of REM and NREM dreams. *Sleep, 13,* 449–455.

Chalmers, D.J. (1996). *The conscious mind: in search of a fundamental theory.* New York: Oxford University Press.

Chapman, R.M., Ilmoniemi, R.J., Barbanera, S., & Romani, G.L. (1984). Selective localization of alpha brain activity with neuromagnetic measurements. *Electroencephalography and Clinical Neurophysiology, 58,* 569–572.

Cheal, M.L. (1997). Understanding diverse effects of visual attention with the VAP-filters metaphor. *Consciousness and Cognition, 6,* 348–362.

Cobb, W.A., & Sears, T.A. (1960). A study of the transmission of potentials after hemispherectomy. *Electroencephalography and Clinical Neurophysiology, 12,* 371–383.

Conway, B., Halliday, D., Farmer, S., Shahani, U., Maas, P., Weir, A., & Rosenberg, J. (1995). Synchronization between motor cortex and spinal motoneuronal pool during performance of a maintained motor task in man. *Journal of Physiology, 489,* 917–924.

Corballis, M.C. (1994). Perceptual integration following commisurotomy: a reappraisal. In M. Sugishita (Ed.), *New Heuropsychology* (pp. 139–158). Amsterdam: Elsevier.

Corballis, M.C. (1995). Visual integration in the split brain. *Neuropsychologia, 33,* 937–959.

Corbetta, M., Akbudak, E., Conturo, T.E., Snyder, A.Z., Ollinger, J.M., Drury, H.A., Linenweber, M.R., Petersen, S.E., Raichle, M.E., Essen, D.C.V., & Shulman, G.L. (1998). A common network of functional areas for attention and eye movements. *Neuron, 21,* 761–773.

Corbetta, M., & Shulman, G.L. (1998). Human cortical mechanisms of visual attention during orienting and search. *Philosophical Transactions of the Royal Society of London—Series B, 353,* 1353–1362.

Corbetta, M., Shulman, G.L., Miezin, F.M., & Petersen, S.E. (1995). Superior parietal cortex activation during spatial attention. *Science, 270,* 802–805.

Coull, J.T., & Frith, C.D. (1998). Differential activation of right superior parietal cortex and intraparietal sulcus by spatial and non-spatial attention. *Neuroimage, 8,* 176–187.

Coull, J.T., & Nobre, A.C. (1998). Where and when to pay attention: the neural systems for directing attention to spatial locations and to time intervals as revealed by both PET and fMRI. *Journal of Neuroscience, 18,* 7426–7435.

Crick, F. (1984). Function of the thalamic reticular complex: the search-light hypothesis. *Proceedings of the National Academy of Sciences USA, 81*, 4586–4590.

Crick, F. (1994). *The astonishing hypothesis.* New York: Simon and Schuster.

Crick, F., & Koch, C. (1995a). Are we aware of neural activity in primary visual cortex? *Nature, 375*, 121–123.

Crick, F., & Koch, C. (1995b). Cortical areas in visual awareness: reply. *Nature, 377*, 294–295.

Culham, J.C., Brandt, S.A., Cavanagh, P., Kanwisher, N.G., Dale, A.M., & Tootell, R.B. (1998). Cortical fMRI activation produced by attentive tracking of moving targets. *Journal of Neurophysiology, 80*, 2657–2670.

Dalkara, T., Krnjevic, K., Ropert, N., & Yim, C.Y. (1986). Chemical modulation of ephaptic interaction of CA3 hippocampal pyramids. *Neuroscience, 17*, 361–370.

Darwin, C. (1859). *On the origin of species by means of natural selection.* London: Murray.

Davies, F.W., Mantzaridis, H., Kenny, G.N.C., & Fisher, A.C. (1996). Middle latency auditory evoked potentials during repeated transitions from consciousness to unconsciousness. *Anaesthesia, 51*, 107–113.

Davis, K.D., Taylor, S.J., Crawley, A.P., Wood, M.L., & Mikulis, D.J. (1997). Functional MRI of pain- and attention-related activations in the human cingulate cortex. *Journal of Neurophysiology, 77*, 3370–3380.

deBeer, N.A., Hooff, J.C.v., Brunia, C.H., Cluitmans, P.J., Korsten, H.H., & Beneken, J.E. (1996). Midlatency auditory evoked potentials as indicators of perceptual processing during general anaesthesia. *British Journal of Anaesthesia*, *77*, 617–624.

Deiber, M.P., Ibanez, V., Bastuji, H., Fischer, C., & Mauguiere, F. (1989). Changes of middle latency auditory evoked potentials during natural sleep in humans. *Neurology*, *39*, 806–813.

Dennett, D.C. (1995). *Darwin's dangerous idea: evolution and the meanings of life.* London, New York: Penguin.

Donchin, E., Callaway, E., Cooper, R., Desmedt, J.E., Goff, W.R., Hillyard, S.A., & Sutton, S. (1977). Publication criteria for studies of evoked potentials (EP) in man. Report of a committee. In J.E. Desmedt (Ed.), *Attention, voluntary contraction and event-related cerebral potentials.* (pp. 1–11). Basel: Karger.

Eeckman, F.H., & Freeman, W.J. (1990). Correlations between unit firing and EEG in the rat olfactory system. *Brain Research*, *528*(2), 238–44.

Elul, R. (1971). The genesis of the EEG. *International Review of Neurobiology*, *15*, 227–72.

Ennever, J.A., Lippold, O.C.J., & Novotny, G.E.K. (1971). The corenoretinal potential as the generator of alpha rhythm in the human electroencephalogram. *Acta Psychologica*, *35*, 269–285.

Eriksen, C.W., & StJames, J.D. (1986). Visual attention within and around the field of focal attention: a zoom lens model. *Perception and Psychophysics*, *40*, 225–240.

Erwin, C.W., Somerville, E.R., & Radtke, R.A. (1984). A review of electroencephalographic features of normal sleep. *Journal of Clinical Neurophysiology*, *1*, 253–274.

Erwin, R.J., & Buchwald, J.S. (1986). Midlatency auditory evoked responses: differential effects of sleep in the cat. *Electroencephalography and Clinical Neurophysiology*, *65*, 373–382.

Faber, D.S., & Korn, H. (1973). A neuronal inhibition mediated electrically. *Science*, *179*(73), 577–8.

Faber, D.S., & Korn, H. (1989). Electrical field effects: their relevance in central neural networks. *Physiological Reviews*, *69*(3), 821–63.

Farrow, J.T., & Hebert, J.R. (1982). Breath suspension during the transcendental meditation technique. *Psychosomatic Medicine*, *44*, 133–153.

Fein, G., Raz, J., Brown, F.F., & Merrin, E.L. (1988). Common reference coherence data are confounded by power and phase effects. *Electroencephalography and Clinical Neurophysiology*, *69*, 581–584.

Fiegl, H. (1967). *The mental and the physical*. Minneapolis: University of Minnesota Press.

Fink, G.R., Dolan, R.J., Halligan, P.W., Marshall, J.C., & Frith, C.D. (1997). Space-based and object-based visual attention: shared and specific neural domains. *Brain*, *120*, 2013–2028.

Foulkes, D., & Schmidt, M. (1983). Temporal sequence and unit composition in dream reports from different stages of sleep. *Sleep*, *6*, 265–280.

Freedman, R., Adler, L.E., Waldo, M.C., Pachtman, E., & Franks, R.D. (1983). Neurophysiological evidence for a defect in inhibitory pathways in schizophrenia: a comparison of medicated and drug-free patients. *Biological Psychiatry*, *18*, 537–551.

Freeman, W.J. (1972). Linear analysis of the dynamics of neural masses. *Annual Review of Biophysics & Bioengineering, 1*, 225–56.

Freeman, W.J. (1978). Spatial properties of an EEG event in the olfactory bulb and cortex. *Electroencephalography & Clinical Neurophysiology, 44*(5), 586–605.

Freeman, W.J. (1991a). Nonlinear dynamics in olfactory information processing. In J.L. Davis & H. Eichenbaum (Eds.), *Olfaction: a model system for computational neuroscience.* (pp. 225–249). Cambridge MA: MIT Press.

Freeman, W.J. (1991b). Predictions on neocortical dynamics derived from studies in paleocortex. In E. Basar & T.H. Bullock (Eds.), *Induced rhythms of the brain* . Boston: Birkhaeuser.

Freeman, W.J., & Baird, B. (1987). Relation of olfactory EEG to behavior: spatial analysis. *Behavioral Neuroscience, 101*(3), 393–408.

Freeman, W.J., & Grajski, K.A. (1987). Relation of olfactory EEG to behavior: factor analysis. *Behavioral Neuroscience, 101*(6), 766–77.

Freeman, W.J., & van Dijk, B.W. (1987). Spatial patterns of visual cortical fast EEG during conditioned reflex in a rhesus monkey. *Brain Research, 422*(2), 267–76.

Freeman, W.J., & Viana Di Prisco, G. (1986). Relation of olfactory EEG to behavior: time series analysis. *Behavioral Neuroscience, 100*(5), 753–63.

French, C.C., & Beaumont, J.G. (1984). A critical review of EEG coherence studies of hemisphere function. *International Journal of Psychophysiology, 1*, 241–254.

Fries, P., Roelfsema, P.R., Engel, A.K., Konig, P., & Singer, W. (1997). Synchronization of oscillatory responses in visual cortex correlates with perception in interocular rivalry. *Proceedings of the National Academy of Sciences USA, 94,* 12699–12704.

Fries, W. (1981). The projection from the lateral geniculate nucleus to the prestriate cortex of the macaque monkey. *Proceedings of the Royal Society of London B, 213,* 73–80.

Friston, K.J., Price, C.J., Fletcher, P., Moore, C., Frackowiak, R.S., & Dolan, R.J. (1996). The trouble with cognitive subtraction. *Neuroimage, 4,* 97–104.

Frith, C.D., & Friston, K.J. (1996). The role of the thalamus in "top down" modulation of attention to sound. *Neuroimage, 4,* 210–215.

Fujiwara, N., Nagamine, T., Imai, M., Tanaka, T., & Shibasaki, H. (1998). Role of the primary auditory cortex in auditory selective attention studied by whole-head neuromagnetometer. *Brain Research. Cognitive Brain Research, 7,* 99–109.

Furshpan, E.J., & Furukawa, T. (1962). Intracellular and extracellular responses of the several regions of the Mauthner cell of the goldfish. *Journal of Neurophysiology, 25,* 732–771.

Furukawa, T., & Furshpan, E.J. (1963). Two inhibitory mechanisms in the Mauthner neurons of goldfish. *Journal of Neurophysiology, 26,* 140–176.

Galambos, R. (1982). Tactile and auditory stimuli repeated at high rates (30–50 per sec) produce similar event related potentials. *Annals of the New York Academy of Sciences, 388,* 722–8.

Galambos, R., Makeig, S., & Talmachoff, P.J. (1981). A 40-Hz auditory potential recorded from the human scalp. *Proceedings of the National Academy of Sciences of the United States of America, 78*(4), 2643–7.

Gastaut, H. (1952). Etude electrocorticographique de la reactivite des rhythmes rolandiques. *Rev. Neurol.*, *87*, 176–182.

Gerard, R.W., & Libet, B. (1940). The control of normal and "convulsive" brain potentials. *American Journal of Psychiatry*, *96*, 1125–1153.

Gescheider, G.A. (1997). *Psychophysics: the fundamentals.* (Third ed.). New Jersey, London: Lawrence Erlbaum Ass.

Gevins, A.S., Doyle, J.C., Cutillo, B.A., Schaffer, R.E., Tannehill, R.S., & Bressler, S.L. (1985). Neurocognitive pattern analysis of a visuospatial task: rapidly-shifting foci of evoked correlations between electrodes. *Psychophysiology*, *22*(1), 32–43.

Giard, M.H., Perrin, F., Pernier, J., & Peronnet, F. (1988). Several attention-related wave forms in auditory areas: a topographic study. *Electroencephalography and Clinical Neurophysiology*, *69*, 371–384.

Globus, G.G. (1973). Consciousness and the brain: the identity thesis. *Archives of General Psychiatry*, *29*, 153–160.

Goldman-Rakic, P. (1997). Space and time in the mental universe. *Nature*, *386*, 559–560.

Graber, B., Rohrbaugh, J.W., Newlin, D.B., Varner, J.L., & Ellingson, R.J. (1985). EEG during masturbation and ejaculation. *Archives of Sexual Behavior*, *14*, 492–503.

Hagelin, J.S. (1984). *Is consciousness the unified quantum field?* Fairfield, Iowa.

Hall, J.W. (1990). *Handbook of auditory evoked responses.* Massachesetts: Simon and Schuster.

Halliday, D., Resnick, R., & Walker, J. (1993). *Fundamentals of physics.* (4th ed.). New York: John Wiley and Sons.

Hansen, J.C., & Hillyard, S.A. (1980). Endogenous brain potentials associated with selective auditory attention. *Electroencephalography & Clinical Neurophysiology, 49*(3–4), 277–90.

Hari, R., & Salmelin, R. (1997). Human cortical oscillations: a neuromagnetic view through the skull. *Trends in Neurosciences, 20*(1), 44–9.

Haug, B.A., Baudewig, J., & Paulus, W. (1998). Selective activation of human cortical area V5A by a rotating visual stimulus in fMRI; implication of attentional mechanisms. *Neuroreport, 9,* 611–614.

Hebb, D.O. (1949). *The organization of behavior.* New York: John Wiley and Sons.

Hebert, R., & Lehman, D. (1977). Theta bursts: an EEG pattern in normal subjects practising the Transcendental Meditation technique. *Electroencephalography and Clinical Neurophysiology, 42,* 397–405.

Hildebrand, J.G. (1995). Analysis of chemical signals by nervous systems. *Proceedings of the National Academy of Sciences USA, 92,* 67–74.

Hillyard, S.A., Hink, R.F., Schwent, V.L., & Picton, T.W. (1973). Electrical signs of selective attention in the human brain. *Science, 182*(108), 177–80.

Hillyard, S.A., Vogel, E.K., & Luck, S.J. (1998). Sensory gain control (amplification) as a mechanism of selective attention: electrophysiological and neuroimaging evidence. *Philosophical Transactions of the Royal Society of London—Series B, 353,* 1257–1270.

Hirai, T. (1974). *Psychophysiology of Zen.* Tokyo: Igaku Shoin.

Hodgson, D. (1991). *The mind matters*. Oxford: Oxford University Press.

Houston, H.G., McClelland, R.J., & Fenwick, P.B. (1988). Effects of nitrous oxide on auditory cortical evoked potentials and subjective thresholds. *British Journal of Anaesthesia, 61*, 606–610.

Ishihara, T., & Yoshii, N. (1972). Multivariate analytic study of EEG and mental activity in juvenile delinquents. *Electroencephalography and Clinical Neurophysiology, 33*, 71–80.

Jefferys, J.G., Traub, R.D., & Whittington, M.A. (1996). Neuronal networks for induced '40 Hz' rhythms [see comments]. *Trends in Neurosciences, 19*(5), 202–8.

Jefferys, J.G.R. (1984). Current flow through hippocampal slices. *Society for Neuroscience Abstracts, 10*, 1074.

Jenkins, B.G., Hill, R., Huang-Hellinger, F., Scholz, V.H., Chen, Y.I., Rosen, B.R., & Chiappa, K. (1996). Simultaneous spectroscopy, fMRI and EEG evaluation of a human ictal epilepsy model: evidence for distributed metabolic hotspots. *Neuroimage, 3*, S601.

Jevning, R., Wallace, R.K., & Beidebach, M. (1992). The physiology of meditation: a review. A wakeful hypometabolic integrated response. *Neuroscience and Biobehavioral Reviews, 16*, 415–424.

Jones, L.A., & Baxter, R.J. (1988). Changes in the auditory middle latency responses during all-night sleep recording. *British Journal of Audiology, 22*, 279–285.

Jueptner, M., Stephan, K.M., Frith, C.D., Brooks, D.J., Frackowiak, R.S., & Passingham, R.E. (1997). Anatomy of motor learning. I. Frontal cortex and attention to action. *Journal of Neurophysiology, 77*, 1313–1324.

Just, M., & Carpenter, P. (1976). Eye fixations and cognitive processes. *Cognitive Psychology, 8*, 441–480.

Kachaturian, Z., Chisholm, R., & Kerr, J. (1973). The effects of arousal on evoked potentials to relevant and irrelevant stimuli. *Psychophysiology, 10*, 194.

Kachaturian, Z., & Gluck, H. (1969). The effects of arousal on the amplitude of evoked potentials. *Brain Research, 14*, 589–606.

Kandel, E.R., Abrams, T., Bernier, L., Carew, T.J., Hawkins, R.D., & Schwartz, J.H. (1983). Classical conditioning and sensitization share aspects of the same molecular cascade in Aplysia. *Cold Spring Harbor Symposia on Quantitative Biology, 48*, 821–830.

Kandel, E.R., Schwartz, J.H., & Jessell, T.M. (1991). *Principles of Neural Science.* (Third ed.). London: Prentice Hall.

Kandel, E.R., Schwartz, J.H., & Jessell, T.M. (1995). *Essentials of Neural Science and Behavior.* Norwalk, Connecticut: Appleston and Lange.

Kaufman, L., Schwarz, B., Salustri, C., & Williamson, S. (1990). Modulation of spontaneous brain activation during mental imagery. *Journal of Cognitive Neuroscience, 2*, 124–132.

Kentridge, R.W., Heywood, C.A., & Weiskrantz, L. (1999). Attention without awareness in blindsight. *Proceedings of the Royal Society of London B, 266*, 1805–1811.

Kohler, W. (1920). *Die psychischen Gestalten in Ruhe und im stationaren Zustand.* Braunschweig: Vieweg und Sohn.

Kohler, W. (1929). *Gestalt psychology.* New York: Liveright.

Kohler, W. (1938). *The place of value in a world of fact.* New York: Liveright.

Kohler, W. (1940). *Dynamics in psychology*. New York: Liveright.

Kohler, W., & Wallach, H. (1944). Figural after-effects: an investigation of visual processes. *Proceedings of the America Philosophical Society, 88*, 269–357.

Konorski, J. (1948). *Conditioned reflexes and neuron organization*. Cambridge: Cambridge University Press.

Korn, H., & Axelrad, H. (1980). Electrical inhibition of Purkinje cells in the cerebellum of the rat. *Proceedings of the National Academy of Sciences USA, 77*, 6244–6247.

Korn, H., & Faber, D.S. (1973). An electrically mediated inhibitory action of the Mauthner cell upon adjacent medullary neurons. *Journal of General Physiology, 61*, 261–262.

Korn, H., & Faber, D.S. (1975). An electrically mediated inhibition in goldfish medulla. *Journal of Neurophysiology, 38*, 452–471.

Kugler, J., & Laub, M. (1971). "Puppet show" theta rhythm. *Electroencephalography and Clinical Neurophysiology, 31*, 532–533.

Kuhlman, W.N. (1978). Functional topography of the human mu rhythm. *Electroencephalography and Clinical Neurophysiology, 44*, 83–93.

Kupfermann, I. (1991). Learning and memory. In E.R. Kandel, J.H. Schwartz, & T.M. Jessell (Eds.), *Principles of neural science*. (pp. 997–1008). London: Prentice Hall International.

LaBerge, D. (1995). *Attentional processing*. Cambridge MA: Harvard University Press.

LaBerge, D., & Brown, V. (1989). Theory of attentional operations in shape identification. *Psychological Review, 96*, 101–124.

LaBerge, S. (1985). *Lucid Dreaming.* Los Angeles: J.P. Tarcher.

Laming, D. (1986). *Sensory Analysis.* London: Academic Press.

Lansing, R.W. (1964). Electroencephalographic correlates of binocular rivalry in man. *Science, 146,* 1325–1327.

Lashley, K.S. (1950). In search of the engram. *Symposium of the Society for Experimental Biology, 4,* 454–482.

Lashley, K.S., & Semmes, K.L.C.a.J. (1951). An examination of the electric field theory of cerebral integration. *Psychological Review, 58,* 123–136.

Laurent, G. (1996). Dynamical representation of odors by oscillating and evolving neural assemblies. *Trends in Neurosciences, 19*(11), 489–96.

Laurent, G., Wehr, M., & Davidowitz, H. (1996). Temporal representations of odors in an olfactory network. *Journal of Neuroscience, 16*(12), 3837–47.

Le, T.H., Pardo, J.V., & Hu, X. (1998). 4 T-fMRI study of nonspatial shifting of selective attention: cerebellar and parietal contributions. *Journal of Neurophysiology, 79,* 1535–1548.

Lehman, D. (1987). Principles of spatial analysis. In A.S. Gevins & A. Remond (Eds.), *Methods of Analysis of Brain Electrical and Magnetic Signals.* (Vol. 1, pp. 309–354). Amsterdam: Elsevier.

Lejeune, H., Maquet, P., Bonnet, M., Casini, L., Ferrara, A., Macar, F., Pouthas, V., Timsit-Berthier, M., & Vidal, F. (1997). The basic pattern of activation in motor and sensory temporal tasks: positron emission tomography data. *Neuroscience Letters, 235,* 21–24.

Leopold, D.A., & Logothetis, N.K. (1996). Activity changes in early visual cortex reflect monkeys' percepts during binocular rivalry. *Nature, 379,* 549–553.

Lippold, O. (1970a). Are alpha waves artefactual? *New Scientist, 45,* 506–508.

Lippold, O. (1970b). Bilateral separation in alpha rhythm recording. *Nature, 226,* 459–460.

Lippold, O. (1970c). The origin of the alpha rhythm. *Nature, 226,* 616–618.

Lippold, O. (1971). Physiological tremor. *Scientific American, 224,* 65–73.

Lippold, O. (1973). *The origin of the alpha rhythm.* Edinburgh, London: Churchill Livingstone.

Lippold, O.C.J., & Novotny, G.E.K. (1970). Is alpha rhythm an artefact? *The Lancet*(May 9), 976–979.

Llinas, R., & Ribary, U. (1993). Coherent 40-Hz oscillation characterizes dream state in humans. *Proceedings of the National Academy of Sciences of the United States of America, 90*(5), 2078–81.

Llinas, R.R., Grace, A.A., & Yarom, Y. (1991). In vitro neurons in mammalian cortical layer 4 exhibit intrinsic oscillatory activity in the 10– to 50-Hz range. *Proceedings of the National Academy of Sciences USA, 88,* 897–901.

Lockwood, A.H., Murphy, B.W., & Khalak, H. (1997). Attentional systems and the allocation of cerebral resources in reading and grammatical tasks. *International Journal of Neuroscience, 91,* 241–252.

Logothetis, N.K., & Schall, J.D. (1989). Neuronal correlates of subjective visual perception. *Science, 245,* 761–763.

Lomo, T. (1966). Frequency potentiation of excitatory synaptic activity in the dentate area of the hippocampal formation. *Acta Physiologica Scandinavica, 68 (Suppl 277)*, 128.

Lumer, E.D., Friston, K.J., & Rees, G. (1998). Neural correlates of perceptual rivalry in the human brain. *Science, 280*, 1930–1934.

MacKay, D.M. (1968). Evoked potentials reflecting interocular and monocular suppression. *Nature, 217*, 81–83.

Maharishi, M.Y. (1969). *Maharishi Mahesh Yogi on the Bhagavad-gita: a new translation and commentary chapters 1–6.* Harmondsworth Middlesex, Baltimore Maryland, Ringwood Victoria: Penguin.

Marshall, C., & Walker, A.E. (1950). The electroencephalographic changes after hemispherectomy in man. *Electroencephalography and Clinical Neurophysiology, 2*, 147–156.

Masland, R.L., Austin, G., & Grant, F.C. (1949). The electroencephalogram following occipital lobectomy. *Electroencephalography and Clinical Neurophysiology, 1*, 273–282.

Mason, L.I., Alexander, C.N., Travis, F.T., Marsh, G., Orme-Johnson, D.W., Gackenbach, J., Mason, D.C., Rainforth, M., & Walton, K.G. (1997). Electrophysiological correlates of higher states of consciousness during sleep in long-term practitioners of the Transcendental Meditation program. *Sleep, 20*, 102–110.

Mataro, M., Garcia-Sanchez, C., Junque, C., Estevez-Gonzalez, A., & Pujol, J. (1997). Magnetic resonance imaging measurement of the caudate nucleus in adolescents with attention-deficit hyperactivity disorder and its relationship with neuropsychological and behavioral measures. *Archives of Neurology, 54*, 963–968.

Maulsby, R.L. (1971). An illustration of emotionally evoked theta rhythm in infancy: hedonic hypersynchrony. *Electroencephalography and Clinical Neurophysiology, 31*, 157–165.

McCallum, W.C. (1988). Potentials related to expectancy, preparation and motor activity. In T.W. Picton (Ed.),, *Human event-related potentials* (Vol. 3,): Elsevier Science Publishers (Biomedical Division).

McEvoy, L., Hari, R., Imada, T., & Sams, M. (1993). Human auditory cortical mechanisms of sound lateralization: II. Interaural time differences at sound onset. *Hearing Research, 67*(1–2), 98–109.

McEvoy, L., Makela, J.P., Hamalainen, M., & Hari, R. (1994). Effect of interaural time differences on middle-latency and late auditory evoked magnetic fields. *Hearing Research, 78*(2), 249–57.

McEvoy, L.K., Picton, T.W., Champagne, S.C., Kellett, A.J., & Kelly, J.B. (1990). Human evoked potentials to shifts in the lateralisation of a noise. *Audiology, 29*, 163–180.

Mendel, M.I., & Goldstein, R. (1971). Early components of the averaged electroencephalographic response to constant clicks during all-night sleep. *J. Speech and Hearing Research, 14*, 829–840.

Mendel, M.I., Saraca, P.A., & Gerber, S.E. (1984). Visual scoring of the middle latency response. *Ear and Hearing, 5*, 160–165.

Michel, C.M., Kaufman, L., & Williamson, S.J. (1994). Duration of EEG and MEG alpha suppression increases with angle in a mental rotation task. *Journal of Cognitive Neuroscience, 6*, 139–150.

Miller, G.A. (1956). The magical number seven, plus or minus two: some limits on our capacity for processing information. *The Psychological Review, 63*, 81–97.

Milner, B., Corkin, S., & Teuber, H.L. (1968). Further analysis of the hippocampal amnesic syndrome: 14–year follow-up study of H.M. *Neuropsychologia, 6,* 215–234.

Mima, T., Nagamine, T., Nakamura, K., & Shibasaki, H. (1998). Attention modulates both primary and secondary somatosensory cortical activities in humans: a magnetocencephalographic study. *Journal of Neurophysiology, 80,* 2215–2221.

Mishkin, M., Ungerleider, L.G., & Macko, K.A. (1983). Object vision and spatial vision: two cortical pathways. *Trends in Neurosciences, 6,* 414–417.

Mizuki, Y. (1982). Frontal midline theta activity during performance of mental tasks. *Electroencephalography and Clinical Neurophysiology, 54,* 25P.

Mizuki, Y. (1987). Frontal lobe: mental functions and EEG. *American Journal of EEG Technology, 27,* 91–101.

Mizuki, Y., Takii, O., Nishijima, H., & Inanaga, K. (1983). The relationship between the appearance of frontal midline theta activity (Fm theta) and memory function. *Electroencephalography and Clinical Neurophysiology, 56,* 56P.

Mizuki, Y., Tanaka, O., Isozaki, H., Nishijima, H., & Inanaga, K. (1980). Periodic appearance of theta rhythm in the frontal midline during the performance of a mental task. *Electroencephalography and Clinical Neurophysiology, 49,* 345–351.

Modrak, D.K.W. (1987). *Aristotle: the power of perception.* Chicago, London: University of Chicago Press.

Morris, R.G.M., Anderson, E., Lynch, G.S., & Baudry, M. (1986). Selective impairment of learning and blockade of long-term potentiation by an N-methyl-D-aspartate antagonist, AP5. *Nature, 319*, 774–776.

Muri, R.M., Felblinger, J., Rosler, K.M., Jung, B., Hess, C.W., & Boesch, C. (1998). Recording of electrical brain activity in a magnetic resonance environment: distorting effects of the static magnetic field. *Magnetic Resonance in Medicine, 39*, 18–22.

Naatanen, R. (1982). Processing negativity: an evoked-potential reflection of selective attention. *Psychological Bulletin, 92*(3), 605–40.

Naatanen, R., Gaillard, A.W., & Mantysalo, S. (1978). Early selective-attention effect on evoked potential reinterpreted. *Acta Psychologica, 42*(4), 313–29.

Naatanen, R., & Picton, T. (1987). The N1 wave of the human electric and magnetic response to sound: a review and an analysis of the component structure. *Psychophysiology, 24*(4), 375–425.

Nagahama, Y., Sadato, N., Yamauchi, H., Katsumi, Y., Hayashi, T., Fukuyama, H., Kimura, J., Shibasaki, H., & Yonekura, Y. (1998). Neural activity during attention shifts between object features. *Neuroreport, 9*, 2633–2638.

Nagel, T. (1974). What is it like to be a bat? *Philosophical Review, 83*, 435–450.

Newton, D.E.F., Thornton, C., Konieczko, K.M., Jordan, C., Webster, N.R., Luff, N.P., Frith, C.D., & Dore, C.J. (1992). Auditory evoked response and awareness: a study in volunteers at sub-MAC concentrations of isoflurane. *British Journal of Anaesthesia, 69*, 122–129.

Niedermeyer, E., Krauss, G.L., & Peyser, C.E. (1989). The electroencephalogram and mental activation. *Clinical Encephalography, 20*, 215–226.

Nobre, A.C., Sebestyen, G.N., Gitelman, D.R., Mesulam, M.M., Frackowiak, R.S., & Frith, C.D. (1997). Functional localization of the system for visuospatial attention using positron emission tomography. *Brain, 120*, 515–533.

Nunez, P.L. (1995). *Neocortical dynamics and human EEG rhythms.* New York: Oxford University Press.

Nunez, P.L., Srinivasan, R., Westdorp, A.F., Wijesinghe, R.S., Tucker, D.M., Silberstein, R.B., & Cadusch, P.J. (1997). EEG coherency. I: Statistics, reference electrode, volume conduction, Laplacians, cortical imaging, and interpretation at multiple scales. *Electroencephalography & Clinical Neurophysiology, 103*(5), 499–515.

Obrador, S., & Larramendi, M.H. (1950). Some observations on the brain rhythms after surgical removal of a cerebral hemisphere. *Electroencephalography and Clinical Neurophysiology, 2*, 143–146.

Ozdamar, O., & Kraus, N. (1983). Auditory middle latency responses in humans. *Audiology, 22*, 34–49.

Palay, S.L., & Chan-Palay, V. (1974). *Cerebellar cortex, cytology and organization.* Berlin: Springer-Verlag.

Pantev, C., Bertrand, O., Eulitz, C., Verkindt, C., Hampson, S., Schuierer, G., & Elbert, T. (1995). Specific tonotopic organizations of different areas of the human auditory cortex revealed by simultaneous magnetic and electric recordings. *Electroencephalography and Clinical Neurophysiology, 94*, 26–40.

Pantev, C., Hoke, M., Lehnertz, K., Lutkenhoner, B., Anogianakis, G., & Wittkowski, W. (1988). Tonotopic organization fo the human auditory cortex revealed by transient auditory evoked magnetic fields. *Electroencephalography and Clinical Neurophysiology, 69,* 160–170.

Pantev, C., Hoke, M., Lutkenhoner, B., & Lehnertz, K. (1991). Neuromagnetic evidence of functional organization of the auditory cortex in humans. *Acta Oto-Laryngologica—Supplement, 491,* 106–115.

Pantev, C., Makeig, S., Hoke, M., Galambos, R., Hampson, S., & Gallen, C. (1991). Human auditory evoked gamma-band magnetic fields. *Proceedings of the National Academy of Sciences of the United States of America, 88*(20), 8996–9000.

Penfield, W., & Rasmussen, T. (1968). *The cerebral cortex of man: a clinical study of localization of function.* New Your, London: Hafner Publishing Co.

Picton, T.W., & Durieux-Smith, A. (1988). Auditory evoked potentials in the assessment of hearing. *Neurologic Clinics, 6,* 791–808.

Picton, T.W., Goodman, W.S., & Bryce, D.P. (1970). Amplitude of evoked responses to tones of high intensity. *Acta Otolaryngologica (Stockholm), 70,* 77–82.

Picton, T.W., Hillyard, S.A., Krausz, H.I., & Galambos, R. (1974). Human auditory evoked potentials. I. Evaluation of components. *Electroencephalography & Clinical Neurophysiology, 36*(2), 179–90.

Plourde, G., Baribeau, J., & Bonhomme, V. (1997). Ketamine increases the amplitude of the 40-Hz auditory steady state response in humans. *British Journal of Anaesthesia, 78,* 524–529.

Plourde, G., & Picton, T.W. (1991). Long-latency auditory evoked potentials during general anesthesia: N1 and P3 components. *Anesthesia and Analgesia, 72,* 342–350.

Pockett, S. (1999). Anesthesia and the electrophysiology of auditory consciousness. *Consciousness and Cognition, 8*, 45–61.

Pockett, S., & Lippold, O.C.J. (1986). Long-term potentiation and depression in hippocampal slices. *Experimental Neurology, 91*, 481–487.

Portas, C.M., Rees, G., Howseman, A.M., Josephs, O., Turner, R., & Frith, C.D. (1998). A specific role for the thalamus in mediating the interaction of attention and arousal in humans. *Journal of Neuroscience, 18*, 8979–8989.

Posner, M.I. (1980). Orienting of attention. *Quarterly Journal of Experimental Psychology, 32*, 3–25.

Pribram, K.H. (1991). *Brain and perception: holonomy and structure in figural processing.* New Jersy, Hove, London: Lawrence Erlbaum Associates.

Pugh, K.R., Offywitz, B.A., Shaywitz, S.E., Fulbright, R.K., Byrd, D., Skudlarski, P., Shankweiler, D.P., Katz, L., Constable, R.T., Fletcher, J., Lacadie, C., Marchione, K., & Gore, J.C. (1996). Auditory selective attention: an fMRI investigation. *Neuroimage, 4*, 159–173.

Rao, K.R. (1998). Two faces of consciousness: a look at Eastern and Western perspectives. *Journal of Consciousness Studies, 5*(3), 309–327.

Recanzone, G.H., Schreiner, C.E., & Merzenich, M.M. (1993). Plasticity in the frequency representation of primary auditory cortex following discrimination training in adult owl monkeys. *The Journal of Neuroscience, 13*, 87–103.

Rees, G., Frackowiak, R., & Frith, C. (1997). Two modulatory effects of attention that mediate object categorization in human cortex. *Science, 275*, 835–838.

Reeves, A., & Sperling, G. (1986). Attention gating in short-term memory. *Psychological Review, 93*, 47–72.

Ribary, U., Ioannides, A.A., Singh, K.D., Hasson, R., Bolton, J.P., Lado, F., Mogilner, A., & Llinas, R. (1991). Magnetic field tomography of coherent thalamocortical 40-Hz oscillations in humans. *Proceedings of the National Academy of Sciences of the United States of America, 88*(24), 11037–41.

Richardson, T.L., Turner, R.W., & Miller, J.J. (1984). Extracellular fields influence transmembrane potentials and synchronization of hippocampal neuronal activity. *Brain Research, 294*, 255–262.

Romani, G.L., Williamson, S.L., & Kaufman, L. (1982). Tonotopic organization of the human auditory cortex. *Science, 216*, 1339–1340.

Rotterdam, A.v., Silva, F.H.L.d., Ende, J.V.d., Viergever, M.A., & Hermans, A.J. (1982). A model of the spatial-temporal characteristics of the alpha rhythm. *Bulletin of Mathematical Biology, 44*, 283–305.

Sagan, P.M., Stell, M.E., Bryan, G.K., & Adey, W.R. (1987). Detection of 60–hertz vertical electric fields by rats. *Bioelectromagnetics, 8*(3), 303–13.

Salenius, S., Kajola, M., Thompson, W.L., Kosslyn, S., & Hari, R. (1995). Reactivity of magnetic parieto-occipital alpha rhythm during visual imagery. *Electroencephalography & Clinical Neurophysiology, 95*(6), 453–62.

Salenius, S., Portin, K., Kajola, M., Salmelin, R., & Hari, R. (1997). Cortical control of human motoneuron firing during isometric contraction. *Journal of Neurophysiology, 77*(6), 3401–5.

Salenius, S., Salmelin, R., Neuper, C., Pfurtscheller, G., & Hari, R. (1996). Human cortical 40 Hz rhythm is closely related to EMG rhythmicity. *Neuroscience Letters, 213*(2), 75–8.

Salmelin, R., & Hari, R. (1994a). Characterization of spontaneous MEG rhythms in healthy adults. *Electroencephalography & Clinical Neurophysiology, 91*(4), 237–48.

Salmelin, R., & Hari, R. (1994b). Spatiotemporal characteristics of sensorimotor neuromagnetic rhythms related to thumb movement. *Neuroscience, 60*(2), 537–50.

Santamaria, J., & Chiappa, K.H. (1987). *The EEG of Drowsiness.* New York: Demos.

Sasaki, K., Tsujimoto, T., Nambu, A., Matsuzaki, R., & Kyuhou, S. (1994). Dynamic activities of the frontal association cortex in calculating and thinking. *Neurosience Research, 19*, 229–233.

Schwender, D., Faber-Zullig, E., Fett, W., Klasing, S., Finsterer, U., Poppel, E., & Peter, K. (1994). Mid-latency auditory evoked potentials in humans during anesthesia with S(+) ketamine—a double-blind, randomized comparison with racemic ketamine. *Anesthesia and Analgesia, 78*, 267–274.

Schwender, D., Faber-Zullig, E., Klasing, S., Poppel, E., & Peter, K. (1994). Motor signs of wakefulness during general anaesthesia with propofol, isoflurane and flunitrazepam/fentanyl and mid-latency auditory evoked potentials. *Anaesthesia, 49*, 476–484.

Schwender, D., Kaiser, A., Klasing, S., Peter, K., & Poppel, E. (1994). Midlatency auditory evoked potentials and explicit and implicit memory in patients undergoing cardiac surgery. *Anaesthesiology, 80*, 493–501.

Schwender, D., Klasing, S., Madler, C., Poppel, E., & Peter, K. (1993a). Effects of benzodiazepines on mid-latency auditory evoked potentials. *Canadian Journal of Anaesthesia, 40,* 1148–1154.

Schwender, D., Klasing, S., Madler, C., Poppel, E., & Peter, K. (1993b). Mid-latency auditory evoked potentials during ketamine anaesthesia in humans. *British Journal of Anaesthesia, 71,* 629–632.

Schwender, D., Rimkus, T., Haessler, R., Klasing, S., Poppel, E., & Peter, K. (1993). Effects of increasing doses of alfentanil, fentanyl and morphine on mid-latency auditory evoked potentials. *British Journal of Anaesthesia, 71,* 622–628.

Scoville, W.B. (1968). Amnesia after bilateral mesial temporal-lobe excision: Introduction to case H.M. *Neuropsychologia, 6,* 211–213.

Searle, J.R. (1993). The problem of consciousness. In G.R. Bock & J. Marsh (Eds.), *Experimental and theoretical studies of consciousness* (Vol. 174, pp. 61–80). Chichester: John Wiley and Sons.

Sergejew, A.A. (1997). *Signal modelling of ECOG maturation in the fetal lamb: tests of a brain model.* PhD, University of Auckland.

Shear, J. (1990). *The inner dimension: philosophy and the experience of consciousness* (Vol. 4). New York, Berne, Frankfurt, Paris: Peter Lang.

Shefrin, S.L., Goodin, D.S., & Aminoff, M.J. (1988). Visual evoked potentials in the investigation of "blindsight.". *Neurology, 38,* 104–109.

Sheinberg, D.L., & Logothetis, N.K. (1997). The role of temporal cortical areas in perceptual organization. *Proceedings of the National Academy of Sciences USA, 94,* 3408–3413.

Sherlock, W. (1751). *A practical difcourfe concerning death.* (28th ed.). London: R. Whitworth.

Shulman, G.L., Remington, R.W., & McLean, J.P. (1979). Moving attention through visual space. *Journal of Experimental Psychology: Human Perception and Performance, 5*, 522–526.

Silva, F.H.L.d., Hoeks, A., Smits, H., & Zetterberg, L.H. (1974). Model of brain rhythmic activity: the alpha rhythm of the thalamus. *Kybernetik, 15*, 27–37.

Silva, F.H.L.d., Vos, J.E., Mooibroek, J., & Rotterdam, A.V. (1980). Relative contributions of intracortical and thalamocortical processes in the generation of alpha rhythms, revealed by partial coherence analysis. *Electroencephalography and Clinical Neurophysiology, 50*, 449–456.

Snow, R.W., & Dudek, F.E. (1986). Evidence for neuronal interactions by electrical field effects in the CA3 and dentate regions of rat hippocampal slices. *Brain Research, 367*(1–2), 292–5.

Sperry, R. (1982). Some effects of disconnecting the cerebral hemispheres. *Science, 217*(4566), 1223–6.

Sperry, R. (1984). Consciousness, personal identity and the divided brain. *Neuropsychologia, 22*(6), 661–73.

Sperry, R.W. (1966). Mental unity following surgical disconnection of the cerebral hemispheres. *Harvey Lectures, 62*, 293–323.

Sperry, R.W. (1968). Hemisphere deconnection and unity in conscious awareness. *American Psychologist, 23*(10), 723–33.

Sperry, R.W. (1969). A modified concept of consciousness. *Psychological Review, 76*(6), 532–6.

Srinivasan, R., Russell, D.P., Edelman, G.M., & Tononi, G. (1999). Increased synchronization of neuromagnetic responses during conscious perception. *Journal of Neuroscience, 19*, 5435–5448.

Stapells, D.R., Linden, D., Suffield, J.B., Hamel, G., & Picton, T.W. (1984). Human auditory steady state potentials. *Ear and Hearing, 5*, 105–113.

Stapells, D.R., Makeig, S., & Galambos, R. (1987). Auditory steady-state responses: threshold prediction using phase coherence. *Electroencephalography & Clinical Neurophysiology, 67*(3), 260–70.

Steriade, M. (1994). Sleep oscillations and their blockage by activating systems. *Journal of Psychiatry & Neuroscience, 19*(5), 354–8.

Steriade, M. (1999). Cellular substrates of brain rhythms. In E.N. & F.L da Silva (Eds), *Electroencephalography: basic principles, alinical applications and related fields.* (pp. 28–75). Baltimore: Williams and Wilkins.

Steriade, M., Curro Dossi, R., & Contreras, D. (1993). Electrophysiological properties of intralaminar thalamocortical cells discharging rhythmic (approximately 40 HZ) spike-bursts at approximately 1000 HZ during waking and rapid eye movement sleep. *Neuroscience, 56*(1), 1–9.

Steriade, M., Dossi, R.C., Pare, D., & Oakson, G. (1991). Fast oscillations (20–40 Hz) in thalamocortical systems and their potentiation by mesopontine cholinergic nuclei in the cat. *Proceedings of the National Academy of Sciences of the United States of America, 88*(10), 4396–400.

Steriade, M., Gloor, P., Llinas, R.R., Lopes de Silva, F.H., & Mesulam, M.M. (1990). Report of IFCN Committee on Basic Mechanisms. Basic mechanisms of cerebral rhythmic activities. *Electroencephalography & Clinical Neurophysiology, 76*(6), 481–508.

Steriade, M., & Llinas, R.R. (1988). The functional states of the thalamus and the associated neuronal interplay. *Physiological Reviews, 68*, 649–742.

Stern, J., Walrath, L., & Goldstein, R. (1984). The endogenous eyeblink. *Psychophysiology, 21*, 22–33.

Stevens, S.S. (1957). On the psychophysical law. *Psychological Reviews, 64*, 153–181.

Stewart, M., & Fox, S.E. (1990). Do septal neurons pace the hippocampal theta rhythm? *Trends in Neuroscience, 13*, 163–168.

Streletz, L.J., Katz, L., Hohenberger, M., & Cracco, R.Q. (1977). Scalp recorded auditory evoked potentials and sonomotor responses: an evaluation of components and recording techniques. *Electroencephalography and Clinical Neurophysiology, 43*, 196–206.

Stufflebeam, S.M., Poeppel, D., Rowley, H.A., & Roberts, T.P. (1998). Peri-threshold encoding of stimulus frequency and intensity in the M100 latency. *Neuroreport, 9*, 91–94.

Takahashi, N., Shinomiya, S., Mori, D., & Tachibana, S. (1997). Frontal midline theta rhythm in young healthy adults. *Clinical Encephalography, 28*, 49–54.

Taylor, C.P., Krnjevic, K., & Ropert, N. (1984). Facilitation of hippocampal CA3 pyramidal cell firing by electrical fields generated antidromically. *Neuroscience, 11*, 101–109.

Tesche, C.D., Uusitalo, M.A., Ilmoniemi, R.J., Huotilainen, M., Kajola, M., & Salonen, O. (1995). Signal-space projections of MEG data characterize both distributed and well-localized neuronal sources. *Electroencephalography and Clinical Neurophysiology, 95*, 189–200.

Thatcher, R., & John, E.R. (1977). *Functional neuroscience. Vol 1. Foundations of cognitive processes*. Hillsdale, New Jersey: Erlbaum.

Thornton, C., Heneghan, C.P., James, C.P.H., & Jones, J.G. (1984). Effects of halothane or enflurane with controlled ventilation on auditory evoked potentials. *British Journal of Anaesthesia, 56*, 315–322.

Tiihonen, J., Hari, R., Kajola, M., Karhu, J., Ahlfors, S., & Tissari, S. (1991). Magnetoencephalographic 10-Hz rhythm from the human auditory cortex. *Neuroscience Letters, 129*(2), 303–5.

Tiihonen, J., M.Kajola, & Hari, R. (1989). Magnetic mu rhythm in man. *Neuroscience, 32*, 793–800.

Tiitinen, H., Sinkkonen, J., May, P., & Naatanen, R. (1994). The auditory transient 40-Hz response is insensitive to changes in stimulus features. *Neuroreport, 6*(1), 190–2.

Tiitinen, H., Sinkkonen, J., Reinikainen, K., Alho, K., Lavikainen, J., & Naatanen, R. (1993). Selective attention enhances the auditory 40-Hz transient response in humans. *Nature, 364*(6432), 59–60.

Tononi, G., Srinivasan, R., Russell, D.P., & Edelman, G.M. (1998). Investigating neural correlates of conscious perception by frequency-tagged neuromagnetic responses. *Proceedings of the National Academy of Sciences USA, 95*, 3198–3203.

Tsal, Y. (1983). Movements of attention across the visual field. *Journal of Experimental Psychology: Human Perception and Performance, 9*, 523–530.

Tucker, D.A., & Ruth, R.A. (1996). Effects of age, signal level and signal rate on the auditory middle latency response. *Journal of the American Academy of Audiology, 7*, 83–91.

Tulving, E., & Schacter, D.L. (1990). Priming and human memory systems. *Science, 247*, 301–306.

Turner, R.W., Richardson, T.L., & Miller, J.J. (1984). Ephaptic interactions contribute to paired pulse and frequency potentiation of hippocampal field potentials. *Experimental Brain Research, 54*, 567–570.

Tzourio, N., Massioui, F.E., Crivello, F., Joliot, M., Renault, B., & Mazoyer, B. (1997). Functional anatomy of human auditory attention studied with PET. *Neuroimage, 5*, 63–77.

Ungerleider, L.G. (1995). Functional brain imaging studies of cortical mechanisms for memory. *Science, 270*, 769–775.

Verleger, R. (1991). The instruction to refrain from blinking affects auditory P3 and N1 amplitudes. *Electroencephalography and Clinical Neurophysiology, 78*, 240–251.

Volkmann, J., Joliot, M., Mogilner, A., Ioannides, A.A., Lado, F., Fazzini, E., Ribary, U., & Llinas, R. (1996). Central motor loop oscillations in parkinsonian resting tremor revealed by magnetoencephalography. *Neurology, 46*(5), 1359–70.

Vvedensky, V., Ilmoniemi, R., & Kajola, M. (1986). Study of the alpha rhythm with a 4–channel SQUID magnetometer. *Medical and Biological Engineering and Computing, 23*, 11–12.

Wallace, R.K. (1970). Physiological effects of Transcendental Meditation. *Science, 167*, 1751–1754.

Watanabe, T., Harner, A.M., Miyauchi, S., Sasaki, Y., Nielsen, M., Palomo, D., & Mukai, I. (1998a). Task-dependent influences of attention on the activation of human primary visual cortex. *Proceedings of the National Academy of Sciences USA, 95*, 11489–11492.

Watanabe, T., Sasaki, Y., Miyauchi, S., Putz, B., Fujimaki, N., Nielsen, M., Takino, R., & Miyakawa, S. (1998b). Attention-regulated activity in human primary visual cortex. *Journal of Neurophysiology*, *79*, 2218–2221.

Weiskrantz, L. (1997). *Consciousness lost and found*. Oxford, New York, Tokyo: Oxford University Press.

White, P.F., Way, W.L., & Trevor, A.J. (1982). Ketamine—its pharmacology and therapeutic uses. *Anesthesiology*, *56*, 119–136.

Whittington, M.A., Traub, R.D., & Jefferys, J.G. (1995). Synchronized oscillations in interneuron networks driven by metabotropic glutamate receptor activation [see comments]. *Nature*, *373*(6515), 612–5.

Whyte, L.L. (1961). *Essay on atomism: from Democritus to 1960*. London: Thomas Nelson and Sons.

Woldorff, M.G., Gallen, C.C., Hampson, S.A., Hillyard, S.A., Pantev, C., Sobel, D., & Bloom, F.E. (1993). Modulation of early sensory processing in human auditory cortex during auditory selective attention. *Proceedings of the National Academy of Sciences of the United States of America*, *90*(18), 8722–6.

Woldorff, M.G., & Hillyard, S.A. (1991). Modulation of early auditory processing during selective listening to rapidly presented tones. *Electroencephalography & Clinical Neurophysiology*, *79*(3), 170–91.

Woldorff, M.G., Hillyard, S.A., Gallen, C.C., Hampson, S.R., & Bloom, F.E. (1998). Magnetoencephalographic recordings demonstrate attentional modulation of mismatch-related neural activity in human auditory cortex. *Psychophysiology*, *35*(3), 283–92.

Wright, J.J. (1997). EEG simulation: variation of spectral envelope, pulse synchrony and approximately 40 Hz oscillation. *Biological Cybernetics*, *76*, 181–194.

Wright, J.J., & Kydd, R.R. (1992). The electroencephalogram and cortical neural networks. *Network*, *3*, 341–462.

Wright, J.J., & Liley, D.T. (1995). Simulation of electrocortical waves. *Biological Cybernetics*, *72*, 347–356.

Xu, Z.M., Vel, E.D., Vinck, B., & Cauwenberge, P.V. (1996). Middle-latency responses to assess objective thresholds in patients with noise-induced hearing losses and Meniere's disease. *European Archives of Oto-Rhino-Laryngology*, *253*, 222–226.

Yabe, H., Tervaniemi, M., Sinkkonen, J., Huotilainen, M., Ilmoniemi, R.J., & Naatanen, R. (1998). Temporal window of integration of auditory information in the human brain. *Psychophysiology*, *35*(5), 615–9.

Yamamoto, T., Uemura, T., & Llinas, R. (1992). Tonotopic organization of human auditory cortex revealed by multi-channel SQUID system. *Acta Oto-Laryngologica*, *112*(2), 201–4.

Yim, C.C., Krnjevic, K., & Dalkara, T. (1986). Ephaptically generated potentials in CA1 neurons of rat's hippocampus in situ. *Journal of Neurophysiology*, *56*, 99–122.

Yukie, M., & Iwai, E. (1981). Direct projection from the dorsal lateral geniculate nucleus to the prestriate cortex in macaque monkeys. *Journal of Comparative Neurology*, *201*, 89–97.

Zeki, S. (1993). *A vision of the brain*. London: Blackwell.

Zeki, S., Watson, J.D.G., & Lueck, C.J. (1991). A direct demonstration of functional specialization in the human visual cortex. *Journal of Neuroscience, 11*(641–649).

Zeki, S.M. (1978). Functional specialisation of the visual cortex of the rhesus monkey. *Nature, 274*, 423–428.

www.ingramcontent.com/pod-product-compliance
Lightning Source LLC
Chambersburg PA
CBHW061405280526
45784CB00001B/373